THE COLLECTED POEMS OF WILLIAM HAWKINS

The Collected Poems of William Hawkins

edited by Cameron Anstee

CHAUDIERE BOOKS MMXV

For my Mother

Always

Contents

Living now In Ottawa: Williams Hawkins at the Margins

I sing:

Ottawa
rivers & jails,
fantasies
the dawn can't
slow up.

—*Ottawa Poems* (1966)

1966 was a good year for William Hawkins. He published two individual collections, was placing work regularly in a number of Canada's emerging little magazines, and had the distinction of appearing in the seminal Contact Press anthology *New Wave Canada: The New Explosion in Canadian Poetry*. The list of contributors to the anthology includes several of the most important voices in Canadian poetry for the following decades: Daphne Buckle, Victor Coleman, David McFadden, bpNichol, Michael Ondaatje, Fred Wah. Hawkins's biographical note ends, "[L]iving now in Ottawa" (171). The dominant histories of Canadian poetry in the 1960s and 1970s pay little attention to Ottawa. Hawkins's declaration (almost confession) of his Ottawa residence places him in the margins of literary history. However, if one looks closely at many of the significant developments of these years, Hawkins is present, not simply working but often forging the path. Though only in his mid-twenties, he was at the centre of a vibrant Ottawa community, and also factored into significant movements in Canadian literature. Hawkins walked away from poetry, at least publicly, in the 1970s. A combination of exhaustion, substance abuse, a growing family, and a sense of disenchantment with the poetry scene led to his early retirement. Hawkins's own silence resulted in a critical silence, resigning his body of work to further margins: out of print, uncollected, and largely unread. However, his various projects (publishing, editing, organizing events, writing) identify, engage with, and pre-figure an astonishing number of the major developments of those fertile years.

His earliest periodical publications came in 1962 (*Alphabet*, *The Canadian Forum*, *Delta*). His work was also being published in collaboration with a number of visual artists in Ottawa as early as 1961. Hawkins, twenty-one years old at the time, worked closely with artists Robert Rosewarne, Fran Jones, Andries Hamann, and Christopher Wells to produce "poster poems," printed on a 130-year-old Washington Press and distributed on telephone poles across the city of Ottawa. These posters were colourful, brash, exuberant, obscene, and large (two feet by three feet approximately). Hawkins's free verse poems were paired with enormous woodcuts and prints, both abstract and representational. The posters were important early sites of contact with the artists who would continue to illustrate and design his books into the twenty-first century. They also point the way to the explosion of concrete poetry that would occur across Canada in the coming years. These visual settings of his poetry are among the earliest examples of collaborations between poets and visual artists in this generation. However, they were produced and distributed primarily in Ottawa, and thus off the radar of the ferment taking place in Toronto and elsewhere. The posters were the aggressive declaration of an art community in an otherwise conservative city, offering a stark contrast to a municipality that had a delayed experience of the freedoms of the sixties.

Postage Stamps

Now in my twenty-first year
brick vaults
function against me

O loomtazark and blip-foo
I think it's the end
people
and I must say something
or do something
So I run thru it all
down the Mall
and Bank Street too
my head covered
with postage stamps
crying
mail me!
mail me!
And the crazy people ask
and where
Billy
and where
And I say
O anywhere

—*Shoot Low Sheriff, They're Riding Shetland Ponies!* (1964)

His behaviour, and the persona that behaviour cultivated, were similarly at odds with middle-class, bureaucratic Ottawa. Although the city bestowed an "Outstanding Young Man" Award on Hawkins in 1966 for his distinguished service in the arts community, his lifestyle was out of step with the image of that award. One of the poster poems, "King Kong Goes to Rotterdam," posted a penis and testicles on telephone poles across Ottawa. Prior to his life as an "Outstanding Young Man," Hawkins spent time in the Val Tetreau Correctional Institution in Quebec for what Roy MacSkimming describes as "some misdemeanour involving other people's cars" (11). MacSkimming, a peer and collaborator, recalls that Hawkins "took drugs, drank too much, insulted important people. In fact he insulted most people, important or not, more or less on principle" (11).

Hawkins regularly wrote poems in which he adopted his "King Kong" persona, an alter-ego of sorts. Describing the series at a reading in 1972, the poet explained, "I sent King Kong all over the world because I couldn't go all over the world ... most of the time I was in ... at the time I wrote these, I was in jail" (*Northern Comfort* 3-4). King Kong was a poetic outlet for the impulses and behaviours that Ottawa could not accommodate the expression of:

King Kong Goes to Rotterdam

Why now King Kong me
Me silent seeker of the Rotterdam of pussycats
Me troubled watcher of St. Orlovsky's bear
I'm in the ice-bags of tomorrow's girl
My endless aspirations of Holland won't save me
I've seen the blond girls of Rotterdam copulating
Oblivious of world sorrow
But ecstatic for corduroy trousers

I wear corduroy trousers
Yet I am a billion miles from pigtails

—*Shoot Low Sheriff, They're Riding Shetland Ponies!* (1964)

In the summer of 1963, Hawkins drove across the country with Roy MacSkimming in a "quaint, arthritic Morris Minor convertible" (MacSkimming 13) to attend the now legendary UBC Summer Poetry Seminar in order to study under Allen Ginsberg, Charles Olson, Denise Levertov, Robert Duncan, and Robert Creeley. The two returned appropriately inspired and immediately self-published a book of poems, the excellently-titled *Shoot Low Sheriff, They're Riding Shetland Ponies!* (1964), making their own modest contribution to the wave of small presses shortly to emerge.

Hawkins's next publication was also a collaborative book, *Two Longer Poems: The Seasons of Miss Nicky by Harry Howith and Louis Riel by William Hawkins* (Toronto: Patrician Press, 1965). Ostensibly published by Patrician Press, it was truly a self-published venture. As with his first book, *Louis Riel* received little attention upon its release. It stands out though, not only in Hawkins's bibliography but in the Canadian literary landscape, for its attempt to take up a historical figure in the service of a long poem. Long poems occupy a central place in the history of Canadian poetry. Dorothy Livesay set the tone for the critical reception of the Canadian form with her declaration in 1969 that what "interests me in these developments is the evidence they present of a conscious attempt to create a dialectic between the objective facts and the subjective feelings of the poet" (267). Ondaatje took up this charge when he edited *The Long Poem Anthology* in 1979, declaring in his introduction that Canadian poets "have to come to terms with the vastness of our place and our vast unspoken history" in ways "personal, transitional, and local" (11). Hawkins, in 1965, states at the outset of *Louis Riel*: "Any divergencies [*sic*] from [the] strict historical account are of my own unconscious invention" (30). This is followed closely by an epigraph from Lawrence Durrell: "What I most need to do is record experiences, not in the order which they took place—for that is history—but in the order in which they first became significant to me" (31). Hawkins's *Louis Riel* exists adjacent to the historical record, in the space between objective fact and subjective feeling identified by Livesay. The poem reads with remarkable prescience given what would follow in Canadian poetry:

> What I had wanted
> have wanted

since the beginning
                    was to speak
from where I am
to where you are
Louis Riel

—*Louis Riel* (1965)

Think of Margaret Atwood's experiments with voice and story in *The Journals of Susanna Moodie* (1970) or Michael Ondaatje's layering of biography, myth, the personal, and the public in *The Collected Works of Billy the Kid* (1970). The historiographic long poem forms a major part of Canada's literary history, and Hawkins's *Louis Riel*, largely forgotten, located that territory years before the major voices of his generation accomplished the same.

Throughout the 1960s, Hawkins was publishing in the most significant experimental little magazines in Canada (*Alphabet*, *Delta*, *Hyphid*, *IS*, *Island*, *Tish*, *Volume 63*, *Weed*) and North America (*El Corno Emplumado*). He published *Ottawa Poems* with Nelson Ball's Weed/Flower Press in 1966, the same year as his appearance in *New Wave Canada*. In 1967, his work was published in *Modern Canadian Verse* edited by A.J.M. Smith, sitting between Margaret Atwood and Gwendolyn MacEwen in the table of contents. Hawkins caught Smith's eye with lyric poems, such as "Spring Rain":

Spring Rain

This black life
this conversing with shadows

& what about reality
or economic aspects,
restricting movement,

halting growth
or the children in a room apart
torturing themselves?

are we not mutations
reconciling diverse things?

is not water
a symbol of life
& this life of death?

is not that haze
before my eyes
spring rain?

—*Hawkins* (1966)

Hawkins was visible in other cultural spheres as well. He was an active member of Ottawa's musical community, playing in a number of bands and helping to operate Le Hibou, an internationally recognized coffee house founded by Denis Faulkner that brought much of the best jazz and folk talent to Ottawa to perform. Bruce Cockburn recalls, "When [I] started writing songs, it was to put music to Bill Hawkins' lyrics" (9). Hawkins played with Cockburn, Sandy Crawley, David Wiffen, Darius Brubeck, and others in The Children and Heavenly Blue. His songs were featured on the soundtrack to the 1967 NFB documentary, *Christopher's Movie Matinee* (the title itself a song of Hawkins's), and were recorded by groups such as The Esquires and Three's a Crowd. He organized and hosted poetry readings by Irving Layton, James Reaney, and Gwendolyn MacEwen, and musical performances by Leonard Cohen, Gordon Lightfoot, and Joni Mitchell. Irving Layton's reading was recorded and eventually released by Posterity Records as the LP *Irving Layton at Le Hibou*, produced and edited by Hawkins with a short essay on Layton by Roy MacSkimming and a sleeve design by Christopher Wells. Hawkins moved easily between poetry and music, refusing to acknowledge stable barriers between the two. The *Ottawa Citizen* described him in 1966 as "Canada's own Bob Dylan" on the occasion of his "Outstanding Young Man" award. Harvey Glatt must be credited here with supporting Hawkins (in terms financial, legal, and moral), as well as nurturing the gradual development of Ottawa's musical and artistic communities through his Treble Clef record stores, concert promotion, and CHEZ-FM most visibly. Glatt's involvement with True North Records must also be credited with the release of the tribute album *Dancing Alone: Songs of William Hawkins* (2008) and *Time Capsule: the Unreleased 1960s Masters* (2013) by The Children.

Hawkins's output slowed following the 1960s, publishing a valuable selected poems with New Press in 1971 (*The Gift of Space* edited by Roy MacSkimming, who was a partner at New Press), a chapbook-length collection with S:A.W. Publications in 1974 (*The Madman's War*), and a book-length sequence in *Anthos* in 1980 ("Sweet & Sour Nothings"), before beginning to reappear in 2005 with the updated selected poems published by Broken Jaw Press, *Dancing Alone*. The disenchantments of the 1970s that contributed to his withdrawal are on display in *The Madman's War*, a book permeated by what Roy MacSkimming describes as a "spirit of exhaustion and futility" (17):

Declaration of Dependence

HAVE LOST MY SMALL WAR WITH GOD STOP I WRITE
THIS SO AS TO SUE FOR PEACE STOP KNOWING UNCON-
DITIONAL SURRENDER THE ONLY TERMS AVAILABLE STOP
I ACCEPT STOP

SEND COLLECT

—*The Madman's War* (1974)

A review of *The Gift of Space* by a. offstein published in *Open Letter* in 1972 suggests something of what Hawkins might have accomplished, and how he might have been received, had he continued publishing regularly. offstein describes *Ottawa Poems* as "the heart" (54) of the selection, "one of the best of its type: A reflection of the city in the historic river, its past in the mind of its present population, symmetrical in construction with a beautiful play of internal rimes, touched off by a surprise ending" (54–55). However, offstein feels Hawkins's work suffers generally for "inconsistency of style and doubtful self-confidence" (52). The promise and ability are clear, and his best work stands with the best being produced around him. Unfortunately, his withdrawal from writing and publishing was sustained. In a 1978 interview in Ottawa's *Sparks Poetry Newsmagazine*, he declared, "I am retired [...] I am 37, but I have been retired since I was 33." "Motive?" asks the interviewer. "Boredom," Hawkins responds. He spent the following decades driving a cab for Blue Line in Ottawa, escorting the wealthy and the poor, artists and politicians, across the city of Ottawa, a city he dragged into the 1960s in his poetry and songs. He retired in 2012.

That same year he was inducted into the VERSeOttawa Hall of Honour, the first poet to receive the honour. At the induction ceremony Hawkins gave a virtuoso reading, performing his earliest poems from memory and delighting the audience with a display full of the humour, energy, and charisma he was known for in the 1960s. Introducing Hawkins at the ceremony, rob mclennan remarked, "William Hawkins is not only from here, but remained here, influencing and celebrating the City of Ottawa during a period that had very few poets known outside of the city's borders, and remarkably few avenues for publication." His is a legacy for Ottawa to be proud of, and his work deserves to be read and remembered across the country.

The Collected Poems of William Hawkins nearly doubles the work presented in *Dancing Alone*, restoring poems that were cut from both previous volumes of selected poems as well as locating a large number of previously uncollected works and adding the small number of new poems Hawkins has written in the intervening decade. This volume includes extensive notes detailing the print history of Hawkins work and provides context where relevant and available. As well, it includes a bibliography of his books, broadsides, periodical publications, anthology appearances, and other items.

The final words of this brief introduction to Hawkins's life and work must, of course, go to the poet. In *Ottawa Poems*, surely Hawkins's most important book, the reader finds the following declaration that encapsulates much of what is best in his poetic output—the poet is sensitive, angry, exhausted, and located tenuously at a limit of personal experience and expression:

I want to toughen
my attitudes
on mediocrity

& make a few statements
on values
to the crowded busload.

I reach my stop
& get off—silent
& frightened by visions
of mad house Brockville
& me in real tears. inside.

—*Ottawa Poems* (1966)

Cameron Anstee
Ottawa, October 2014

Works Cited

Cockburn, Bruce. Preface. *Dancing Alone: Selected Poems*. By William Hawkins. Fredericton: Broken Jaw Press (cauldron books 5), 2005. 9.

Hawkins, William. *Shoot Low Sheriff, They're Riding Shetland Ponies!* with Roy MacSkimming. Ottawa: [n.p.], 1964.

--. *Two Longer Poems: the Seasons of Miss Nicky by Harry Howith and Louis Riel by William Hawkins*. Toronto: Patrician Press, 1965.

--. *Hawkins: Poems* 1963-1965. Ottawa: Nil Press, 1966.

--. *Ottawa Poems*. Kitchener: Weed/Flower Press, 1966.

--. *The Madman's War*. Ottawa: S.A.W. Publications, 1974.

"Interview with William Hawkins." *Sparks Poetry Newsmagazine* 1:11 (January 1978): n.p.

"Jaycees Honour Young Men's Achievements." *Ottawa Citizen* 24 November 1966. 43.

Livesay, Dorothy. "The Documentary Poem: A Canadian Genre (1969)." *Contexts of Canadian Criticism*. Ed. Eli Mandel. Chicago: University of Chicago Press, 1971. 267-281.

MacSkimming, Roy. "William Hawkins: A Unique Voice in Canadian Poetry." *Dancing Alone: Selected Poems*. By William Hawkins. Fredericton: Broken Jaw Press (Cauldron books 5), 2005. 11-18.

mclennan, rob. "William Hawkins introduction for the VERSeOttawa Hall of Honour Inductee Ceremony." *rob mclennan's blog*. 25 March 2013. Web.

Northern Comfort. Ottawa: Commoners' Press, 1973.

offstein, a. Rev. of *The Gift of Space: Selected Poems 1960/1970*. *Open Letter* 2:2 (Summer 1972): 52-56.

Ondaatje, Michael. Introduction. *The Long Poem Anthology*. Ed. Michael Ondaatje. Toronto: The Coach House Press, 1979.

Weiselberger, Carl. "Of Dadaism, Nietzsche and Zen Buddhism (... And Ottawa Artists in Search of 'Life' Amid Clutter of Creativity)." *Ottawa Citizen* 20 February 1962. 17.

Shoot Low Sheriff, They're Riding Shetland Ponies!

(1964)

Cathexis

Along the shore line
Of this vast sea Cathexis
Tides roar, paced by evil moon
And parched by moral sun
And the grains of coloured sand
Which I now am stirring
Are ever changing, ever multiplying

And I too need soldiers.

King Kong Goes to Rotterdam

Why now King Kong me
Me silent seeker of the Rotterdam of pussycats
Me troubled watcher of St. Orlovsky's bear
I'm in the ice-bags of tomorrow's girl
My endless aspirations of Holland won't save me
I've seen the blond girls of Rotterdam copulating
Oblivious of world sorrow
But ecstatic for corduroy trousers

I wear corduroy trousers
Yet I am a billion miles from pigtails

Postage Stamps

Now in my twenty-first year
brick vaults
function against me
O loomtazark and blip-foo
I think it's the end
people
and I must say something
or do something
So I run thru it all
down the Mall
and Bank Street too
my head covered
with postage stamps
crying
mail me!
mail me!
And the crazy people ask
and where
Billy
and where
And I say
O anywhere

Two Short Ones

I am told that pigeons
or birds of some sort
shit all over Beethoven's statue
in Vienna
I used to like birds
now
I just don't know
what to think

. . . .

My friend Hamann is painting the end of it all
It's all square to him
and I don't understand
I tell him
in an elaborate manner
that I don't understand
and he is elated
My friend Hamann also likes birds
and me and Ludwig
find that hard to take

Child

for Andries

Bright eyes of pussycat
a plague on deceit—
you brand new sparkler.

O playpens on drunk afternoons!
Dreams of Egypt!
& death unknown in your imagination of cookie

Child, give me your hand.

The Vision of King Mountain

Surrounded by the myth of big men
And the reality of girl-boys
                                                I
                                        neither big man or girl-boy
Stand alone in the Autumn-exhausted hills
Praying for rabbits
                                    hating the cold
                        and wishing that the obvious vision of King Mountain
                            would reveal itself to me

And yet I am unable to climb to the peak of that mountain
Where all visions are possible
I stay over the automobile-slain body of a rabbit
Trying to draw an insane line of relation
From the big men to the girl-boys to the dead rabbit

I am a child of Autumn
See the orange in my eyes

Xochiquetzal

A flower saddened by the grief of years,
Zoned by trees, impaled on three-pronged Spanish spears,
To you, Xochiquetzal, my marriage song is sung,
Epithalamium for a much suffered and suffering one
Caught and bald-headed with fear on the Heaven ladder's final rung.

Whiteness of wave and mountain top are in you, you Mexico harlot and
Hermetic child of tears. And I see the white sand
On your seasoned bed.
Reach bony fingers for the guilt-flung pesos as they
Eclipse the smouldering eyeholes in your head

King Kong Goes to Saudi-Arabia

While King Konging in Saudi-Arabia
Watched patiently by millions of Saudi-Arabians
Now definitive King Kong monster
To the unravished and mysterious Saudi-Arabian chicks
Of veils and confusing sheets
Who whisper in giggles of King Kong failures in Rotterdam
And points south

I Grand Prophet and Procrustean Peer of Monsterism
Practice weird voodoo and cabbala magic
Dreaming of a fixed Prime Ministers' Conference
With everyone under my evil spell
Ending in orgy of London Streets
Where at last King Kong believed in
By London urchins and fair maids

O England! Home of Monsters!
Of you I dream!
I tell Saudi-Arabian Horrors of your empty coal mines!
I tell them of your tubercular scraggly-haired loud-mouthed women!
O England! Guard your dragons!
Feed your vampires!
One day we shall all King Kong thru the streets of Stratford!

A Song of Flowers

Flowers of sadness and of evil
Flowers of the parlours and fields of the dead
Flowers of my Granny dead in a hospital
I do not wonder at your disappearance
Winter is on this land
Laying down endless quilts of quiet sadness
Flowers being good flowers must die in sadness
No flower can be born in sadness
And never ever a flower bloomed in sadness
        lest of course it be a nutty and unserious flower
A flower of the songs of man

Porsche

for H.G.

If I had me a Porsche
A black sleek animal Porsche
I'd find me a brick wall
With two miles of road in front of it
and
    BANG
        me and the Porsche would swing out

For Jenny Louisa Lockyear

"Duerme, vuela, reposa: Tambien se muere el mar!"
Lorca

You holy and now dead old woman
You who so loved Rupert Brooke
and cried for him
annual tears
speaking softly to me of wars
and the ultimate adagio of death
You who read me Tennyson reluctantly
And James Whitcomb Riley digging every line
You who played with me from your wheelchair
Shooting your great gun
a cane
How bloom Yeats' roses this year, old one?
Can you smell them?

Birth

Tomorrow Child
you bring
Another explosion of daffodils
To ring your entrance of pain.

And crocuses
mad at eternity
With the promise of fleeting Spring.

Of these flowers I can say nothing;
But of you Tomorrow Child
I can say you will resurrect me
Even before I die.

And the flowers
fragile and lovely as even you
Will one day be smashed beneath your flying feet.

Tallahassee

Because I have never arrived, never met you,
I find it impossible to imagine my ever leaving.
And tho I do not know you
with your Joe Palooka dreams
& Humphrey Pennyworth realities
& cannot yet say your tender name
still I dream fantastic sonnets of death history
your death history
a hallucination of my wildsad mind
in proximity with Huey Long's mad dream of a rebuilt White House.

Swept clean once in the beginning
by the knives and dog teeth
of the children of Europe—
Naked & trembling your ass to the world like some
young
nubile girl
of rivers forgetful
tho you pulsed with desire
for the Sea—
You, Tallahassee, represent my America
And to represent the all of one thing is horror
then the mar of the whole must be in you.

O Tallahassee why were you not just
the ripe breast of America
bared to nourish starving travellers
from Butte Montana

Why not this alone?
Why also the gangrened thighs?

Tallahassee, Tallahassee, the slow freight from Memphis is arriving—
with Hart Crane
water-logged & sea-weary
crouched behind an awful door.

Billy Graham Goes to Tallahassee

Strange man
with your Heaven-afflicted eyes
burning this night
thru sinful Tallahassee
Exhorting & pleading & haranguing the multitudes
like a
Southern John the Baptist,
Did you see your living Jesus
(for he shall rise up from among you)
walk down the aisle
his beard full of salt and crabs
Whispering soft plans for *your* crucifixion?

Woman from Tallahassee

Too bad you are not here with me now
but gone, gone to Tallahassee
            to work in a coal mine

tubercular, scraggly-haired and loving rice.

I dream inside your rotting lungs and know
ultimately why Tallahassee
            and wonder if you will be able to get
the eyebrow and lash replacements there
            needed badly if you continue to fight

the reality of the sun!

O woman! Heat hoarding Cracker! That coal will diamond and blind you! Thunder will come heralding the end of you and Tallahassee too while under the crumbling ruins inspired maggots scheme fantastic new things!

The earth will reverse itself
                                    three times
                        and then come water
                        bringing forth you, naked,
                        with all ugliness washed away
                        and all life too.

A Monster's Travelogue

Concerning King Kong, aspirant Monarch of England, pussy-footing rogue in Rotterdam & Cabbala Leader in sandy Saudi-Arabia, as he travels to Tallahassee

BOOM! BOOM! BOOM! BOOM! BOOM! BOOM!

Battered & ball-wracked, immense pilgrim snug in his cups of Horror,
King Kong with his nowtime fantastic followers:
Saudi-Arabian spiced & dreamy women—
Turtle eggs & weird chants of Cabbala admirers—
Whores from Holland in reluctant tow—
And sad & lonely tuberculosis of England waving a futile Union Jack—
"I arrive like many another before
"Syphilitic on America's shore."

"O Mason-Dixon Line I lie snug below you!
"O bayou hiding places!
"Plans of conquest! The crackers with their ears filled with dirty wisdom!
"Black-skinned memories of Mau Mau!
"Sad gentlemen in wicked wicked Virginia!
"And a final plowhorse of Tallahassee with leather eyes,
"Suspicious of Alabama & Louisiana!"

"Whole political systems based on the words of Uncle Wiggly!
"My childhood monster hero!
"I have come to absorb you!
"Damns that are dams of overflowing milk!
"The ultimate kindness of abolished zoos!
"Texas Texas Texas!
"I tell you Tallahassee the smell of female sweat is stronger than that
of juniper or magnolia
"And you will never be a New Orleans!"

My Darling

My darling laid down her head
she laid it down—smoking!

She ate grass & complained of ivy.

She saw transatlantic cocks in soup.

And watched the fairies romp
                    on the green green grass
                    & worried about the dew.

She did   I saw it
& the precious dew too.

The Lament of Tom Mix

O spurs of Destiny
Don't jab my ass—
Give me one more chance
To nail em at the pass!

Dream of Father

for Richard Thomas

I saw you last night
lifting the anxieties of winter
perpetuating the hoax of summer—
O song of Father
to a springtime-autumn boy.

When will we decision eternity?
Or build that bridge
that bridge you promised me
of song & automobiles
outside the realm of dream?

Late Nite Vision

Shiva & that other cat are dead
A new being
both dancer & dreamer
rules

What shall I
of dancer against flowers say
or of the dreamer
on that high hill
learn from you
the flowers

who created him.

Story Time

for Jenny

You speak to me
& tell me stories
of your various selves.

I do not mind,
my story of you does not change.

I stay
hoping my story
will begin
after you stop talking.

Fire Girl

Fire it was
she brought
in the cold & the wet
oppressive cold & wet

Fire it was she was
a wall of it

breaking … breaking …

& then
            people
the flood

The Fire

The fire held me, I know,
guided me, placed me in your secret parts.
You are asleep now,
little animal,
the fire out.

But not so for me,
I rage yet!
Ignited tinder, I whisper,
inflammable substances!

Love & imaginings
flicker
I am a camera
disgusted by the grind
the wheels
celluloid
exhausted by what I see.

I expect, soon, to stop seeing,
grow silent
& listen.
I will record your every heartbeat,
learn the secret of your breath
& discuss your freckles with my friends.
Do you toss now?
I am beside you.
I'm being clinical about all this.
Can you stand it?

Suffer, stupid bitch,
but never fear—
for you

tomorrow is just another dream.

Louis Riel (1965)

Preface

I wish to acknowledge as source for the historical data, *Louis Riel* by Brig. George F. G. Stanley. Any divergencies from his strict historical account are of my own unconscious invention.

William Hawkins
Ottawa, October, 1964

"What I most need to do is record experiences, not in the order which they took place—for that is history—but in the order in which they first became significant to me."

Lawrence Durrell, *Justine*

Prologue

But they enter,
he said,
differently—
sceptical
& know, somehow, what they will see
or what they will choose to see;
love even.

Sure, I said,
but I enter dancing,
innocent of that life
& not fearing Know.

& I care
I do
I care.

Part One

What I had wanted
have wanted
since the beginning
                    was to speak
from where I am
to where you are
Louis Riel

        the prayer then
        being that you
        would be there too
        with me
not under grass, in Deadtown, disgraced—
nor drained of meaning by Time—
nor translated into some other world, not open to me—

        but here, here!
        before me
        where I could know you
        call your name

& talk of that
your Destiny
when we arrived at that one place.

What if he had known
or intuited
standing over Scott's body
the discharge of four guns only
making that death slight to sound
with the sun shining bright
& the "superior" *anglais* blood flowing

that that event
would lead him to 1885 death
& more for him: disgrace
even a mother could not alleviate.

Or of Schultz thought long
who escaped him & roused
Toronto the Good
against his Métis
April 6, 1869

& wished for him dead
instead of simple Scott.

Of him Macdonald said:
"If we get him here
"he is a gone coon."

& Macdonald, that man of biblical verbs,
often praised & revered & dear father called,
seemed not to comprehend the Red River business,
was not aware of what went on;
had no name to call it.

On that same day, April 6,
Abbé Ritchot & his companions,
negotiators for the Settlement
& therefore Riel,
arrived in St. Cloud, Minnesota,
& took trains & other means not known to me
heading for Ottawa.

> Who did not know
> but must have feared
> that they would be arrested in Ottawa
> with bleak Toronto warrants
> charging them with Scott's murder
> much to the satisfaction of the Orange.

That they did fear arrest
or at least hindrance
their different routes
(Ritchot via Buffalo
& Judge Black via Detroit)
surely shows.

& after their release
talks &
the priest, Ritchot, being firm
& Sir John infirm,
he, Macdonald, chucked the whole to Cartier
& went on a bender.

Cartier gave assurances
but no papers
& the same from Young
had Ritchot worried
but not enough.

& Schultz spread rumours,
rumours of Scott buried alive,
the blood running from his true chest,
firing Protestant Ontario with plans of revenge.

A piece of rope
Scott's hands supposedly bound with for his execution
was sent from Schultz to Denison

who told the latter to show it at meetings
& suggest there that Riel be hung with it
their victory assumed over him
& his death sure
therefore.

Of the military operation rumours
Ritchot learned nothing,
but Macdonald, it is known, wished Her Majesty's Imperial Forces
& not Canadian troops
to give show of strength on the Red River,
thus intimidating Riel they hoped—

as surely they would.

But Her Majesty's Government
was inclined to let Macdonald stir his own brew
& keep it from boiling over
with Her but prepared
to eat of it.

But what of his mind,
the thoughts in it when finally aware
that Ritchot had not known Toronto
& its influence
& that Cartier's hands were tied
even on promises
& that death *could* come before the amnesty.

The Bishop Tâché
on his own hook
travelled east to obtain in writing
what Ritchot had by mouth.
No wonder indecision ...
troops coming without pardon,
Tâché not heard from ...

        & so flight
        then the horses wandering off
        the lost shoe
        cold cold cold
        all minor compared to bitterness of possible,
        maybe apparent, defeat

tho he mumbled about the Manitoba Act accomplishment
& that he considered his work finished

        still he went to his mother.

In the Settlement
Goulet dies
drowned—hit on the head with a rock

escaping bloodthirsty Canadians
he sank …

& others:

François Guillemette, beaten to death;
Bob O'Lone, the same;
André Nault, beaten & left for dead;
even Father Kavanaugh, not man of Riel, nearly done in.

All in the name of Scott.

Provincial elections—him out—fear of Orangemen the reason—fear for family & province's peace also a consideration.

Ending in illness
near to death
seeing Angels

While O'Donaghue plotted
with Fenians
his comical conquest plans.

In 1871 Sir John sent Bishop Tâché $1,000 to be paid Riel over a twelve month period so that he would be able to leave the country & Smith added $600 to that. So that Macdonald could say to the electorate: "Where is Riel? I wish I could lay my hands on him."

Part Two

"Poetry and History, it seems, must always be a little at variance."
Victor Hugo, *Notre Dame de Paris*

Ah my good Louis
good for yet another day
& I am still with you—

with you
& your insanity
in Ottawa
            a fine place for insanity—
tho I have said nothing of that
it will come

            & of your love speak
            if the spirit moves me
            & of your associates & enemies
            & their actions more must I say.

& that he stood down
in Provencher
          for Cartier
asking nothing for himself
but expecting that mythical amnesty
& good treatment for his people

          & Cartier
          I recall
          before even assuming office
          up & dies
          & Louis elected again.

He went to Ottawa
& with hip moves
signed in
as Member of Parliament.

          Ottawa aghast.

Orange Lodge attendance swells.

          Louis Riel! Louis Riel!

But did not sit in Commons

          & Schultz
          that bastard again
          had him expelled.

While Lepine

that great giant
gets nabbed for murder

Scott again
that much murdered man.

& with Lepine

Nault, whom they had tried to kill before
& Lagimodière—

Scott's ghost
working hard.

Louis during this time
at odds with the cosmos

first signs.

That amnesty
when it came
of a bastard sort

    banishing him
    freeing Nault
    & the others
    from the noose

the straw that finally broke him.

I call witness to his Washington D.C. visions:
God in a cloud, he like Moses, only humble, more humble than,

    he imagines.

His duties outlined,
his instructions received,

    like those of his mother
    God telling her to marry
    that first Louis Riel, the father,
    noble man.

& he then as trilogy
as history:

    the Count of Chambord
    Don Carlos of Spain
    & himself.

March 6, 1876,
yclept by others Louis R. David,
which he denied promptly—

he knew his name
was not to be denied that as well—

admitted
warm with terror
to the Hospital St. Jean de Dieu.

(Manitoba followers
did they know
were they shattered,

& what about mother?)

People in hospital, staff members,
all images to him:

> Sister Ste-Thérèse:
> "Image of the House of Austria."
>
> Dr. Howard:
> "Image of Protestant Russia."
>
> Dr. Lachapelle:
> "Image of blackest Liberalism,"
> also represents Bismarck
> be it noted here.

The hospital then
merely an attempt
to drive the Holy Spirit from him.

Then, because of Orangemen in the mind,
taken to Quebec City Funny Farm,

there remaining
until January 23, 1878.

For two years he ran the corridors, naked,
striking mad blows for freedom.

& called himself: Louis David Riel
Prophet, Infallible Pontiff & Priest-King.

& plotted moving the Holy See
from Rome to Montreal.

He did.

What was done to silence his visions
not known

    perhaps he just played it cool,
    kept them to himself,
    waiting for the release
    which came

& he dreamed of solitary farms in Nebraska
after it.

Part Three

"always beware the leader
who talks with God
and leaves you to do the dirty work."
Raymond Souster, *Place of Meeting*

Evelina
& me reluctant to deal
with that
as you were even tho far way, Louis,
in Montana.

What can I say here?

That he stayed with her family
& had secret engagement
& he wrote verses
& she excited about his life?

> (but where, I say,
> could you have gone
> little French girl
> in what streets wander,
> hand-holding, with that man,
> Louis Riel?)

but later betrayed
& confused about love therefore
& he married
an illiterate
Métis

& roamed with her
seeking divine buffalo
who knew the various secrets of currency.

Montana
marriage
the return of vision

        & his mission soon to move North-West
        he did not know it
        like Stefansson's
        theory on Empires almost

Louis all hung up
teaching school
when he *knew* revolt
had schemed impossible victories—

        doomed this event.

In the Spring of 1883
it was
he taught school
& heard the knock on the door

> travelling 700 miles
> Saskatchewan Métis
> need Louis Riel

& in 1884 he took it up again,
he the chosen took his mission
up as he took them
his family up
& he went North-West.

The New Catholic Empire
flashing his brain
& from his brain
& rising up in holy flame
from flat prairie brush.

The Indians meeting too
big councils
throughout the country
all wondering about his mind.

& they in Lorne
not like the Indians their relatives
had no man to say stop
or go

who but Louis Riel
could they turn to?

& so they went to Montana
& God spoke
in whispers now
to him & he came
that agitator, Louis Riel.

& the word
spread
thru the prairies: Louis Riel!

No Orangemen in this tale now.

Now you're a prophet, Louis,
for real
& I am lost, unable to move with you,
with you man of motion of spinning.

You're all wheels, Louis,
& find myself going the way of Ritchot
that good man
into stunned silence.

I knew from that first battle
(dead: 12 Horsemen & five of yours)
watching you, unhappy that blood would flow,
holding the cross that helped you prophesy victory,
that in the East 8,000 men volunteered to kill you
& many of your own deserted.

But what of your prayers
do they count for nothing here on my balance sheet
not of judgement
but of knowing
that you could pray for even Macdonald, who said:
"Riel will hang tho every dog in Quebec barks."
& worry about children.

Can I not move
again
from this point
inward
move!
as I have moved before?

To get in close to you
in tight where I could talk as the others did not
to tell you of death
to tell about numbers
about history & heroes.

But what's the use?
your madness
your changing the names of the stars
changing the zodiac to rid it of pagan meanings
putting all the priests in South Saskatchewan under surveillance ...

That I have failed is known,
that that earlier part could be justified I never doubted
& that knowledge would be the gap between us ...

But Louis in Christ's name for sure
90 year old men fighting the Mounties
all for your fucked up visions,
lives but glass in your kaleidoscope!

Epilogue

Heroes are Destiny's errors
I said to him
fearing Know—

a melodrama
until the real change;
a partnership of
ideal & reality.

& I said
goodbye—Louis, goodbye!

Hawkins (1966)

To "The Children"
at the gate
demanding entrance

The Only Flag

Our mornings indict us.
I have seen it in your eyes,
stark as streets swarm
with sterile savages.

I have no one but you
& you none but me—
& Baby the mathematics of it
are frightening.

Let's go back to bed
lie down together
& forget our fears,
hearts pounding
to the rhythm of love
& your flaming hair
our banner
for that brief moment.

November 17, 1963

This day I shall note
as my British day,
for love sleeps with other men
& I am unconcerned.

But mull over my affairs
real & imagined,
a sad piper for a distant
ridiculous Queen,
I court her favours
desiring thighs
instead of titles
& see her ass
on all my imaginary dollar bills.

Excuses, Excuses

You must remember
that love you now
is not for all time
nor could it be

& that that fuck
that was thrown
from the centre field of fear
is but a thing in time

& time, which I am involved with
(as a dimension, as a limit
to my imagination)
rains down harsh words on love
on me—
            & I am free
            & stand in wonder once more.

Put Down

Don’t go down to the river, Love,
bad things
happen there
why just yesterday
a man changed

        change comes
        envelops one

even rocks
I hear
change

& if rocks
make it
why not I
for I want that brightest star
& I’ll get it
if somebody
doesn’t try to stop me

        shut up
        go to sleep
        are you crazy
        or something

The High-Flying Eagle

for W.R.

I know you, Eagle,
have seen you flying about.

What is it you want from me?
Poems? Proof
of conscience?

Fly away now,
I am tired,
my supper is cold
& I can't stand about watching you
always …

Peg's Dream

The House has three floors.
It is a warm
well-lighted house.

On the fourth floor
relatives
(all dead & dusty)
wander amidst huge furnishings;
from the rear of the house
near the stairway
we stand
& listen
as they wail their defeat
at the living.

This Thing

From where you stand
the whole thing is different,
not, I feel, as it should be.

Yes, the Angels of Mercy are there—
I see that.
But they are supplicating you.
It's all clearly outlined.

My picture is not so.
I don't feel superior or anything,
nor do I demand you change.
It's just that I thought I should mention
this thing between us.

Autistic

A re-ordering
or placing
of objects in the mind ...

one begins choosing
or switching selves
from the ideal to reality

or lying down
in a room
I know:
          outside
          ladies in girdles
grotesque   ludicrous

men lined up
& applauded
& it appeared ...
no, it was
as if a game
were anticipated

I don't know the rules
but I have assurances
from many sources
that it doesn't matter

Maidanek

My memory is of skulls
charred remains
of possibilities
& accumulated ash.

I cannot explain
what will not be comprehended,
a collective anguish

thousands of shoes
better explain missing feet.

Four Songs of Experience
(I Ching)

I

First toss
& head is rapped
by its perspective

        vision
        or comprehension
        forced into
        a retired brain

Not to stop
believing
in water
or movement without thought

        No springs
        gush forth
        from the much-heralded ground

        it seeps
                & the abyss
                is filled

in time

2

In my own context
I have accomplished
what I could

If the rains come
before harvest—
& it is said they might—
I will be absolved

the Elders
are not
in my context

I am indicted
by falling rain

3

After completion
the analysis
of strength
                        & its locale
& so with weakness

                        caution
                        climax necessitated

At the beginning
no winds blew
& things went well

Now the wind howls
(mouth of deluge!)
papers are blown about
(motherless of Heaven!)
I am much disordered
& cannot sleep

4

Death is unimportant
because imperative

                or the imperative
                permanently
                displayed
                becomes meaningless

(fallen) I
maintain
I am the world's host
who falls
also
I will endeavour
to entertain

                I am waiting

Gratefully
I note
our pit is dry.

Evidence of Mutations, Changes, Etc.
(I Ching)

I

In that consultation
change is the aggressor

a chance
happening
while the mind sleeps

(no fear
the revolving
isms of being)

there too
heroes are discovered
Princes & Ministers
of great Beauty

coins have
carried the
evidence of their passing—

Is the yarrow
broken
stemsnapped
by the pathside
to the yamen house
where there is no yarrow?

words have
sought the
place they,
the changes,
sought

I am word & coin

I am water on the mountain
I am Prince & Minister
I am the missing yarrow …

2

I followed the river
as was dictated
until it became
a tributary
until it became
my loss of the sea

I sat down
in a pre-arranged place of light
& there too sat one I had rejected,
Atatarho, Snake-Man,
Make of Magic & Mystic
& he said:

"Fuck off, you said,
to & give out
wooden nickels
I'll go to find
the sea—
& the distances
shrank for me
as yours increased
& I plotted not
to find,
I sought nothing,
I remained,
for here is peace
& knowledge of the sea
is in a drop of water
shining in the sun."

A New Light

For seeing, a
brightness within,
a luminous centre

for knowing
where to see
where seeing is—

the movement
beyond the darkened window,
beyond the yard
is seized;
it returns knowing all along
that's me, yes,
there I am,
there too.

Revolt

As for lying down
in front of a train
or canoeing into an atomic
submarine

    is as much
    like dying
    with an english hardon
    (curved slightly inwards)

as living with one

    whatever
    any of it means
    I don't know
    I just live here

Letter

I have parted
with reality,
with words as conveyances,
name what I have occult
or hidden

        I hide from it myself
        as it hides from you.

I am aware
of the mess, repressed,
inside your head,

                the conflicts
                reality imposes

The cards told me
& knowing, I endure

                am almost happy.

The Creation Game

Somehow
this is different
& my catalogue of words can't handle it.

Pose, movement
& preparation,
these are the same.

& yet
I am aware of you,
am in you—
my pleasure is in your pleasure.

I feel like a god.

I am a god,
your ecstatic face
my first creation.

Spring Rain

This black life
this conversing with shadows

& what about reality
or economic aspects,
restricting movement,
halting growth
or the children in a room apart
torturing themselves?

are we not mutations
reconciling diverse things?

is not water
a symbol of life
& this life of death?

is not that haze
before my eyes
spring rain?

For David

Why tell the man
the tree (it falls!)
is beautiful

        or that the
        sea is a motion
        its breaking a deception
        or the harbour
        a violent elemental manifestation
        of confusion.

Part of the motion
equal in bearing responsibilities,
is the return
you have called breaking—
all motion returning
into itself.

As a melody is not broken it revolves,
becomes itself

        again & again & again

Impressions of a Mythical Being

I

How is it
in this contest of form
you fall on your ass
& yet win all the prizes?

It must be illusion,
your words: am I not man?
the vibrations from your head.

If I am a continual question
you are an endless answer.

2

Anyone knowing more—pass this.
Anyone knowing less—the same.

(Chanting)

In puja
mantra Hosan-i-Sabbah
Hosan-i-Hosan-i
Sabbah-old man-
mountain-pleasure-
retaining those
who would amputate-
in time-open doors-
the music out-the foliage-
flowers-trellis me-
in time-Horror guru-
cannabis sativa
numquam perit-
sweet scent in head-
last illusions-
the myth of self-in-time-
in puja
mantra Hosan-i-Sabbah!

3

What are the forms,
the repetitions, at night,
the mandala in sleep in motion,
the becoming that ends with
dawn?

illusion?

Always the questions,
hammering, until the rhythms fail
& stop
unanswered.

Grasping it,
having to embrace it,
also the stupidity it registers
left in my hands, damp:
what to do
with preconceptions?
& then the stunning beauty
as the world's green skirts
drift past

& I sleep
but am not
unaware.

4

Real as a rhythm, a notion of power,
now a windowpane you are
light shines thru,
then a morass of pity.

The song
quick to lips
the cry of
roses
taunted
by their thorns

& the change
is in the knowledge
in the need
to change
in the alternative
to change

the death
of dust
where no
stirring winds
blow.

5

that I might return, ahead
to the beginning,
as the back of the garden continues
into the front,

note the changes
eternity has made,

made over
not by time
but timelessness,

& flowers
are still dying,

& the turtle
is still on his back,

& I am
is still doubtful.

Youth

laughs against the April rain,
where nothing ages
nor grows old with grace

here, where age
is covered
with illusions.

Here is no wisdom
just the rain,
the rain falling
& mingling
with unshed tears.

Reply

I don’t know
the rights & wrongs
of what I am
nor your categorizing
of the essential
me, my hang-ups
with history / not vision
are vision / what does it matter?
What I see,
feel, is not really
there, I guess,
unless you see it too?

The Wall

I'm up against the wall,
up to the coarseness,
surrounded by it.

I have imagined the wall,
am responsible—

you'd think,
it is reasonable
to assume
I know what it's for,
but I don't.

I'm painting the wall
green & blue
predominate,
figures shimmer elusive
& I name them.

I'm up against the wall,
I'm part of it
almost, in it
almost, a figure shimmering;
but I don't belong, I don't fit,
for it but not of it
I'll stick around
to see what happens.

Schoenberg

Long-drawn, long tone out-
side my ear, extended regret
bubbles up &
out & down
& in. The song
lonely, the cry
real as the
mechanism conveying it.

Truth is a convenience
few of us
can afford—
the music is really
everywhere cornering
the day's quota of lies
& will be soon working on tomorrow's.

The Seed

there, lilac
heavy hung,
falls freely where it may
& has eyes for blooming
after becoming.

I too am of
seed, fell,
I did, grew
to blossom.

Far mutated, father,
but a blooming thing nonetheless.

Pounding on the Front Door, Coming in the Back

The poem is a rhythm, a syncopated
vibration, called up from the mind,
required for some purpose, some meaning.

I've lost the reason
for the rhythm, have discarded
the excuses & meanings as unnecessary.
& the sounds have become subtle,
not announced to me.

I cannot tell you the why,
just the is, the
rhythm there, rhythm
transposed, or torn out from,
if you must have meaning,
from melodies, the heart of,
too sad to sing.

Mysteriensonaten No. 1

for Maestro

To do the beautiful
thing, without hesitating,
is best confined to art.

More so to anticipate
your destruction
in art
& never life.

The firecracker
in a world of bombs
waiting for the right moment.

Mysteriensonaten No. 2

Being *in* (strange form of: to enter),
for your relation to the present,
the time continuum,
is a happening.

We say, we knew,
knew all along,
we were *in*
& everyone else out.

Knew certain stars
shone brighter too,
tho smaller
they were … & that others
hoarded their light
hopeful of a future.

Mysteriensonaten No. 3

Fragments, all I have, the chips
of the block, the truth
in my words, of it.

You must find your
own words, & breath
for the words,
for it.

Your common walking,
your movement of limbs
is haughty, your
smile, in sunlight,
in the growing garden,

what happens
when night falls?

& the chill sets in?

Mysteriensonaten No. 4

a bird can't lie
his song, wouldn't
want to, can't, doesn't
know how to sing
for nothing
but song.

One hundred & fifty crazy
Dutchmen play
Mahler into the open summer
night, the heart
of German-Jew-Man frustration
a melody no bird
could every sing

but it's song
just the same.

Fragment of a Conversation

for Elizabeth

The same refrain, the
continuances as we sit
& analyse our
defeats, noticing how
they oppose one another.

Perhaps we both
shall receive a seedling
letter, instructions on Hope,
from a becoming missionary
of the ideal world.

But we have nourished
intellect on the truth
& now it is reluctant
to accept substitutes.

Getting Up: A Glimpse of the Poet-Anima in the Nude

(Hero) : Therefore to myself
give comely thanks & praise,
& again, conqueror,
the day gleams forth.

(aside) : Another boatload of shit
sitting in the stagnant harbour.

(Hero) : It is to my everlasting
disgrace: I lie
more to myself than others.

(aside) : Another boatload of shit
sinking in the stagnant harbour.

A Long Strange Question Answered

What's wrong with the moment,
brain time-charged,
unable to function—inward—
the words all wrong, it's final,
wrong they are, as with lies,
as with illusions,

I'm tumbled by
it, the great fiction

I am to people, to self.

Outward is a different trip,
not a made place, not a thing
prepared, outward
is being there, belonging
in all, attitude
to the conflicts
raging, blissful
& head down, eyes open
for mouth to speak for ears to hear
for open eyes to see

a new myth of beauty.

What He's Waiting For

Always returning
to his original terror,
life, the doing it once more,
breaking bread,
the meaningless gestures,
changing his death,
not the reality of it,
not inevitability of it
just the motive.

When the lungs dry up,
he says, when the blood stops
flowing, when the hands curl
inward, you enter
into yourself
& start all over again.

He's still waiting.

Poem for Leo

With nothing to fear
but fear, reality
just a glimmer from a tea
pot, full, & daysold
& at breakfast noted.
I'm noting the necessity
of tragedy in tea
pot drama.

When the shit
we have shat
comes back, return
who'll get
Leo's share, Leo Lion,
big cat, see, his soft claws,
his hunger …

Leo's?

Hello Leo, don't bug me man,
I can't make all this hunger,
makes me fat stomach ache,
you sitting around eating your own shit

every day every day every day.

Ottawa Poems (1966)

"Finally, though he knows himself to be above nature,
he understands that his operations succeed to the
degree that his thought, word and action transmit
faithfully the powers of the plane above him."

Paul Foster Case, *The Tarot, A Key to the Wisdom of the Ages*

I

Toward a story, often
a dream in my head, some trip on power
I'm always returning to, towards
a realization of the dilemma,
the pretension of definition

these actual lines of
a life, from it to you
(the forming force)

standing before you
his words for it: the city,
the funny man.

Subject & object
buggering each other.

2

To Indians
canoeing the Ottawa
a bleak sight, of rock
& tangled shrubs—
a nightmare of growth
clinging to the mountside,

today tourists flock
to peer down

& some
still see Indians
canoeing the Ottawa
digging the bleak sight, of rock
& saying no thanks—

see, they paddle on.

3

The Funny Kind of Prophet Speaks

Fucking, my dear, you observe
yourself fucking me,
not me fucking you, nor we fucking we.

Or involve yourself with life
through that strange motion
& not so strange rhythm—
like the poems in all our heads, never written,
& that rhythm is past,
present & hopefully the future,
is involved in our creation,
prepares or drains us for death.

When the Heavenly Blitz starts
(the script reads) cities will
explode from the massive rhythm
of us all
trying to get one more in(to)
ourselves, each other.

4

What had she, Queen Victoria, in mind
naming this place, Ottawa, capitol?

Ah coolness, he said,
who dug coolness.

The crazy river-abounding town
where people are quietly
following some hesitant
form of evolution
arranged on television
from Toronto.

Where girls are all
possible fucks
in the long dull summernights

& Mounties more image
than reality.

5

how can I describe the anger
a filled bus overcomes me with
or to, how to, justify
hatred of fellow man?

Just one of those
impossible but frequent
happenings …

I want to toughen
my attitudes
on mediocrity

& make a few statements
on values
to the crowded busload.

I reach my stop
& get off—silent
& frightened by visions
of mad house Brockville
& me in real tears. inside.

6

words the song of birds
insists he, bird words
the song is bird's words—
the words of birds.

outside they sing
(jesus christ I know) words of
the birds, just not of words, not of them,
the words just …

outside they are singing
those bird words.

7

A Mild Effort At Philosophy

Things disappear fast,
are gone, I'm trying
to replace them as fast
as I can—the plants
in the garden, the no longer familiar
cat, past loves
& even despair.

Generally, the past
is more difficult
than the future.

& I don't know
what I can say
about my lack of either.

& the present,
too immense,
provide me one more ending,
but no hint at which way
to begin.

8

Poem in Red Ink

Having formed
over time,   an
attitude of mistrust

plus an intimate
infatuation
with my own continued existence,

I decide red
& think bed

go to mine
for sleep

9

A Stupid Canasta Poem
for Saunders

Hold yourself above the images
of beauty, keep clear
of any such attempt at permanence.

Go down on the images
you bear, recall desire

as someone shutting
the bright light off

& tho the ladies may twitter
at offers of head
at least you, down going, are in perfect bliss
trying to fill
an intellectual inside straight, knowing
that losing doesn't change much of anything
if you don't take the game too seriously.

10

Hey there don't
go, a tragedy is shaping
inside my head.

        & there's a fire somewhere burning

        a man's dreams
        I am told
        just down the street
        burning.

Tragic the death of dreams,
memories of Atlantis,
the symbol, transformed to myth,
lying, used, under the couch,
in Heaven, light streaming from it,
we often don't see.

Some kind of new Viper
is playing drums

as the day finally ends.

II

Your hair electric, on legs &
traces on breasts, skin tone,
sly ripples of pleasure,
distant explosions
in my ears & always
a burning within
& me lost in my own confusions.

You see I am not inclined
to discretion,
can offer only
obvious love
to all beautiful people—
at night your silence
keeps me awake.

12

The city extends
no hand to me—
leaves me be.

The frogs I hear are
croaking for something, some meaning,
because I catch their desire.

I am a catcher of desires,
I have been alone
& now love dalliance of the self.

Because of that, the loneliness,
having no one to speak to—
sitting containing
the desire—I send love to all,
screaming it, while the
actual police begin
a pattern of fear
in ever narrowing circles.

13

So much of me is not
beautiful, so much …
my grammar for instance
& I don't know the value
of my words,
constantly, you said, pouring from my head

& they, the words,
are maybe patterns, from dreams,
from my deep sleep.

I wish you could know me
on some mornings, inside some moments,
& I flash my twenty-five years
on a pretentious five second page
like so & am complete.

Tortured, I said,
by our potential
to realize beauty
within & without.

14

Sunday, the small square,
ordered in it, a three-year-old boy,
strangely mine (both resent it)
coaxing some unheard-of melody
from his harmonica.

I, distracted being,
cannot get in tune
but will not let my ego
make judgements
any longer, forced acceptance
of song everywhere
I sing & say
so that's a G harmonica.

& the kid blows a rift
out of his lonely soul, turns me to glass,
me & all my pretensions about meaning.

15

Ah shit don't shoot I'll sing

I sing:

Ottawa,
rivers & jails,
fantasies
the dawn can't
slow up.

I sing:

for song,
Ottawa,
you know nothing
of poems
& you are poems.

I sing:

Buses & poison,
actual criminal exhaust,
people are falling
victim to their conveniences

the man
vibrated to death
by an electric toothbrush.

& me
don't I take drugs?

Listen Ottawa, I can't sleep

seem to have forgotten
the ancient art,

expect too much—
the grey truth of
dawn, now happening,
gives incentives
but it's too late.

Can't you tell me a story?
Get me into one more day?

16

"Beauty will not wait"

will not pause
tho I must name it, locate
its area, will not wait
for the namer to compose
himself

as the river
will not, nor
birds on their
particular branches,

nor my memory of China
wait.

You see the sun floods up
forcing the concerns of day
upon me & upon this night
I've spent with old answers
for everyone's new questions—
the rays of light
announce themselves
& simultaneously
the hammering transcription begins,
the unpoetic aspect of breath begins.

17

Love, classic form of: to please

ejaculations, how many
did it take to build
the Rideau Canal,
how many Saturday night two dollar bangs?

Listen I'll ask the bus driver
this very morning
how often ...

we must have
some norm, some understanding.

Listen, don't feel old
because of love, glibness
or casual fucking is tiresome.

Listen, one day I'm going,
someone will come & take me away.
For smoking shit or pissing on the
War Memorial. For something
they will come & take me.

Who's to say we don't love them
& their cruel ways?

18

I can't, we don't,
they do.

Grammar lessons
on a river bank
he gives grammar
instead of beauty

knows nothing
about either.

The beauty remains,
they will make it—
only he, strange I,
then unrelated pronoun,
leaves—

see him waving goodbye.

19

Homage to Batman

Suddenly there were seams
in my mind

        I seemed to hear
        Batman

feel the acid of his mind.

Remembering forgotten stars,
distant nights,
playing the Joker's crazy & dangerous game …

Something about the failure of past rhythms
driving new tunes out of my head.

20

The Last Poem for People

The heart speaks (to ear, ear to mouth
& mouth to brain) & the tremour
seeks an answer—

(in my bitterness
I offer:

if it is your wish
to be clever, as if to entertain
or to add that
to flight
or flower, as in soul
fading

or without ambition
to rehearse & propagate & to construct
within a group of despairs …)

To see birds fly over the heart
to see water for flowers fading
to see defined men standing together
forming opposing words …

but this is poetry.
The people in the streets are not involved.

& yet sing the isolated garden song, they,
& the lonely mountain,

the dancer whose dance is a distraction,
whose dance is mad, distracting herself
& me & my song I've yet to really sing.

21

Sorry, This Is It

You bring me back to the poem,
your movement marks the periphery
I stand upon tonight. Perhaps (counting ways, verbs)

the sun will change
the beauty of night flowers
& the stars I see in you
will seem less bright then

but this is no concern of mine.

You I am disenchanted that I cannot
speak in symbols about what's
happening, also me not loving
what I cannot touch, a vile man
in vile times, they say of me
'his mind is a mirror dark things groom upon.'

but do not believe Gypsies
now no word but
you is in mind.

I is trying to give an apple back
to a laughing Serpent
somewhere in the Near East.

I don't think he'll be back.

22

You in the morning

You in the morning,
I wanted to do you totally, more than
ever,

    in the evening, often I can't
    & often I never can as I
    would like, to

charge time with love.

Origin of something I have never
carried water in

    you confuse me with feelings
        I can't name,
        can only affirm

& everybody's a Trojan Horse
filled with tender & vicious weapons
& no openings, no
apparent openings.

23

Hello from the Shadows

for Christopher Wells

of the mind & the universe …
the mind, its power is in
the substance of
its object, cosmos, or form—
from without: structure

a time-resisting thing,
contemplating the alley's sacred stone,
my life of ceaseless repetitions,
pointless gestures, initiate
to the magic power of breath,
of symbolic form-structures,

poor product of nature, acting
upon what wisdom I have,

I say hello from the shadows
to you, passing on the street.

24

Characterology

"the dominately sacred
centre—" navel, the navel is the embryo
of character or personality

This was
the story of The Indian astrologer
seeking the point
under the serpent's head
(of the Heavens)
& it supports the world
& on that spot
goes the foundation
of a temple.

But that spot moves
as all things move,
as navel to body moves,
so nothing endures without animation,
acting in lock-step with its gods, with
what has gone before, & there's nothing happening
because its happened. Words
force creation consciousness upon us.

"I am Heaven you are Earth"—
where's Hell but in our minds?
Lie down together, let us on the ground
as the rains fall, we shall lie, fall,
slaking thirst
of the ground we lie on.

We justify our excesses
by the excesses of our gods,

"I will parade
naked through the streets
proclaiming the sorcery of the navel."

Even these actions a participation in what is
sacred at the centre
where I am slowly turning
around a dominately sacred moment of being.

25

The Last Train to Narcissus

I

the thing measured, you did, our thing,
in an eye stare measure, after it was
valued, potential for comprehension
noted, & after we had turned down
the noise all around,
a gentle goodbye fell

(My lips have formed
words for the thing
which I will relate one day
in song).

Follow feeling inside,
or the slaughtered moments out, we are
tears falling, we rage …

& these words a response or reaction
to a manifestation within
slowly winding out.

2

the struggle remains unseen,
in the dark, nobody says
much about it

    ring yourself round
    with roses in the magic
    garden, thorns
    about the navel to protect,
    to cleanse with blood.

Brood on the alternatives
to struggle, weight the gamble,
the dice may never return, may
for ever roll on …

the afternoon falls like passion's
trousers & I illustrate the dark
for you, closing in

    with my knowledge of thorns

adept at instinct
I carry your bags aboard that last foolish train.

26

Almost a Poem

for Robert Hogg

forms are worn away
by recognition—the structures we
have erected begin to age,
symbolically we
extinguish fires,
place new fires, new ash
side by side,

vain heads talking
against appearances
of reality, no light
without & no belief
within,

"I am he who performs
holy work, manifesting
into from

& new men
will learn that possession
is not an act of creation."

unceasing rehearsal
of myth (begins
each day as does
ekpyrosis: universal combustion myth

Conscious of cyclical
duration I see life
as ritual

this is my actual myth,
my meaning in behaviour as a last grasp at Being.

Expert on chance occurrence,
as best I can, explaining,
giving form, the eternal etcetera
sings his song.

27

Books on Iran Wanted

or conversations with the hip Arab who says
No more prognostications,
people, your *polis* is happening

& it's all therein
this unmentionable

Ten Steps Up Or Down

0-	is of course for	(Aleph)
1-	who makes it happen in context	(Beth)
2-	who changes the context	(Gimel)
3-	who cradles my head	(Daleth)
4-	who takes care & reconnoitres	(Heh)
5-	who binds	(Vav)
6-	us as we should be	(Zain)
7-	is power, is consciousness outward	(Cheth)
8-	is power, is consciousness inward	(Teth)
9-	is keeping it hid	(Yod)
10-	is laughing & starting over	(Kaph)

This here is a world of marvels.
Also stern values.

& these moral things, easily acquired,
are hard to use,

spend a whole life
learning when to say
good or bad
                at the wrong times

& being lonely as a poet.

Give this meaning as you may, or must,
at 5.36 a.m. this 6th day of April, year 1966, the sun rose

for me, for you

28

You there are no more endings, beginning now I won't accept them

(in my dreams women
are mandalas—
four ins & four outs)

You there is a window with light shining thru & shades just won't stop it

(around me an order
occurs, I feel
it fall back into place)

You now it's quiet & the clock is ticking out of time,
& nothing but vague ideas are suitable, giving form away
I breathe onto glass & direct traffic in the empty street

(you don't know what it is
to have complete control
over nothing)

So I'll write a song
about this boy & a sleigh,
a sleigh & a boy
with no hill
to go down on.

The Gift of Space: Selected Poems 1960/ 1970 (1971)

For Jenny Louisa Lockyear

"Duerme, vuela, reposa: Tambien se muere el mar!"
Gabriel Garcia Lorca

The Stupid Saint

Silent as a reversal of life
she loving & cancelling out death considerations
in nocturnal moisture

& dying may wait
until you finish
with this misery, this result
of negative diverse laws
I can never explain
without my hands
on your skin.

Wilful Murder

for Bruce

The Saint knows you're a deviate
        & is alarmingly candid about it.
The Saint cannot tip-toe & giggles
        tactlessly while trying.
The Saint plants geraniums & puts down roses
        with a deprecating smile
        & a word about thorns.
The Saint is sure he's right
        & everyone else merely
        intelligently wrong.
The Saint doesn't care about anybody
        except everybody.
The Saint likes himself
        & thinks everybody should
        & he likes them all alphabetically.
The Saint saves his snowballs till July
        hoping for a laugh.

He should get it.

A Gift for Caesar

As if I could sing up
all we've lost—
you mentioned ten days
& I couldn't understand
a simple span of time.
Not like that,
not just like that.
Recently confusion
marks my every step
& my hands, wanting for nothing,
seldom move.

If you desire
come on here to me,
hand-holding
in a place of no delight,
in flickering fires
that cannot dispel
the cold of night,
we'll remain
yours

Mother, the Angel of Death in My Deams

And if existence is only half of existence,
the bad half,
arising hungover & soul
crazy because oh
how his heart
would sing
if he were other than a coward
all the living time.

Funny how
in all the defences we
build, the patterns
we exquisitely form,
none protect us against
the Great Enemy within.
Perhaps the only & lonely
Angel of Death in my dreams

(all seen in the Ides of March,
toy-brained Caesar will always reappear
to witness the great triumph
of his death, *Et tu, Baby?*
his new final sob.)

A Poem About Tomorrow

I do not speak
to make you suddenly silent
as if the distances
between us advertised
the nice guy,
sold as ultimate hog
to hungry millions.

What words fly
in a last offering
to the silent gods!
I have learnt I am a thing,
a sold item
I can't name or even describe.

Some other time
when what is is naught
I'll die whipped out
& famous as a relic
of shrinking promises;
a pet drowned in water,
an animal zoo
charmed by the lines
of manageable movement
in all I love,
in all I'll never be.

A refreshment
taken after midnight;
the concealed listener
whose colour is bad
tunes in the dismal radio
each ethical night.

Before She Could Do It

Before she could do it
she imagined herself do it
to herself

& before she could let me do it
she imagined herself let me do it
to herself

To this day, believe me,
she has never made it
to herself.

A Powerful Cat

for Mort

I speak hoping I know where you
think I am.
Disagreement is inevitable
on a mechanical level.
& what is ill-considered
about defence?

On the loose I speak
in passing,
if I'm not here I'm hiding
beyond the mountain of bad karma
I call my gift to the world.

Paper Roses

When a common rose gave up the secret
of blooming & dying:
there should be no alternative
to beauty—
a small part of uncompromised self
to be carried in a pocket
or in a valise
or amulet.

Words are as common as shit
& often equally aromatic.
I like to fling them about
hoping to fertilize
a couple of dozen literate roses
just for you Witches.

The Gift of Space

The hortative
in blank paper
me wife gives
                    & I'll have to fill it
                    with confetti
                    for all the

little Neddies
how they do flit about
those lovely things we had.

This badly made
from scraps of pity;

a world's pulse
within a held breath
& then gasp, the final
lung or needle or whatever
gone to support the great good time
we're not having.

The Warner Mystique

Pause in front of light
as it falls off the bulb
onto us, & marvel.

Thus it is with light
& I would have it be with me,
falling on you
from all possible angles.

Projective Tulips

The Queen of Holland
laid them on us,
all the active colours

as put, ordered,
spaced within sensitive
Canadian mediocre
arrays   plurals they are

along a stagnant canal.

To think then they
feel at home, cozy in European jam:
crowd—(big group of diversely
coloured things)

amidst the human debris.

At night the tulip
colour, splashing against the dark,
lights up the love,
the caring of the young

backsides answering
the pulse & flux
of the stars
as they go to it.

Learning lessons
silent flowers only say
& teaching me
yet another way
to see

Expanded Translation of a Half-Remembered Haiku

love is a song tropical fish sing
at my house in the morning.
a song fish sing & we're so
stoned we can't hear it.

no you are not a bad woman,
just a silly one. we are
never so beautiful as when lost
& there are things
we all can see. learn to lose,
the Tao is apparent
& winning simply isn't possible.

A Delineation of Memories

a procrastination for Sheila

I

Venus I flash & jerk evocative lines as you
move to enter me. Start then the search,
find me lost brother & twin. Lady Sphere
in an avalanche of brothels come to find us,
shopping for love in flesh supermarkets,
mainly unconscious of beauty
as I go along we are.

I'll admit to wondering what has happened
to my dreams, my hopes
for the long ascension, & whatever it means
to be beyond the limit of this scene,
this fatal human context.

You die because you're alive. & always.

2

In Mars often the disagreeable
guilt afflicts me.

(in my separation
from my lust-mad
family, my horde of dead advisors.)

Who is master of the night, daughter?
My little witch & spawn of lizards—
I now conclude
as a midget in a giant's cave
left with delusions of grandeur
& not even one fantasy outlet
to plug into.

I flirt with my tendencies
& aspire to love.
All my permissions are yours.
I haven't any lies to tell.
I play with instant rules & still lose.

3

In Jupiter I publish
in defiance of my unpopular profession.

I prophesy death
& smile as you wonder
what I'm trying to invent.

I write about what I get into. I did not invent
death. The concept exists. I can't remember
when I'm lying. Often I simply don't care.
Incest does not frighten me, I am an impossible
brother my sister
if you love me as you do.

He masters his destiny who learns to laugh
through his tears, he who looks long
at the stars
knowing only wisdom produces lasting miracles.
Words are decisions the mind makes,
real self-hood is beyond any decision, Cancer
lady & my friend.

4

ringed I find you ringed as if to
ring me you would within you
& there's nothing I can do but hope.

Saturn, if resourceful
resolve my tedious affairs—
for we here are ringed in non-matter
& are naked before a universe of incidents.

You are as I call you & what I see
as you fall, or when ascending
a secret place of the gods, not caring
about up or down. A feminine
thing, a hidden thing
suspiciously watery.

I turn light off to on
reaching no conclusions for improved sight.
Seeing less I must
worry more as this day ages. The clock is singing.
The cuckoo is alive with me
but both being unaware
we proceed with caution …
before such cosmic machinery
we seem as cogs to be found within a purpose
not entirely our own.

5

Uranus my body too keeps a time.
I've studied my own electricity,
have become self-telepathic
in my dualities.

Even though mesmerized by aerodynamics
I grow tired
of unfavourable criticism
by long-dead brethren.

I wish to be free
of tense, alive with the
strength of a moment,
the immediate power
of all temporary things.

The Warlocks of Night don't admit to good or bad.
The Warlocks of Night say we've all been had.

Mr. Gurdjieff won't you please come home?
I volunteer to be used by life,
to continue the long experiment
in relays, if need be.

6

Neptune, poet, as this house is Muse Manor,
is as myth was,
you dwelled in water
because your ears burned with self-deceptions.

You coach me each time I hide
in the rules of games I'll never play.
Can't you see I'm crazy and useless to designs?

Rumours of diffusion,
a panorama of lies, with things I can't tell anyone of,
and leave me with a conversational capacity
but little to say.

My darling Virgo, avoid carelessness
until I am well again, can think again.

Invocation

When Magus sings the people listen.
His song is often theirs.
Lacking a concept of gender,
he will lead the sexy street
to occupy the song.

Magic is what you know
for sure.

Feel it in my hands
as I try to hold us
& don't know what to say.

Weather Report

As befitting a fool
of such stature
I must scribble
something, show
how alive I am.

Cosmic cannibals
are coming
and they are, they are
going to gobble up all dead things
regardless of previous tradition
or precedent
and I bet they gobble up
half dead things too.

A planet can
evolve beyond a need
for fertilizers.
Death the vomit
of new life laws—:

have you noticed how it's getting
colder again?

Stormcentre: Cassandra

Don't worry about enemies
in the middle of this storm.

Hold me tight.
We'll go laughing. (Maybe.)

Abyss, abyss, where am I
when you need me?

Walking the line
with Cassandra—:
we search each other's eyes for fears
and copulate like demons.

Cassandra's Communication Network

I can't be serious on the telephone
cable of your fears. Fly lady
off that wire.
We'll swirl and die in the open air
and inhabit our dubious destiny
with a grace
communication disallows.

Cassandra on a Bender

So inclined to standards are the traitors
they turn her eyes out from the beauty within.
Hecate, the blossom you gave
this sister's eyes
has withered in the heat of unknown passions.

On the brink
with a drunk
she takes a gulp of red wine,
spilling polka dots on her perfect breasts.

Cassandra's Explicit Sacrament

I call it holy and scoop up my fool's remains
and even that falls from my hands—
sexless Mercury.

I call it holy and cannot approach it
outside of madness—

I'm going away tomorrow.

Σατάr

Gallivanting satyriasis: she says
I've got it. Satyrion, an aphrodisiac:
made from orchis (**όρχίε**, greek is fun)
tea from bulbs, O uberous teats.

Sir William Herschel discovered
Uranus, 1781: Neptune—even
farther out—discovered by Galle in
1846. Now who is Galle? Don't know.
Sir Wm., however, was a Scorpio.

Priapism, she now accuses me.
Horrible Torves, no more
do I quiver. Ugglesome Torves

I say orchis bulbs. Not too
neoteric, however, but quite a buzz

On His Thirtieth Year

The rain is darkening, heavy;
I have watched it cancel out the garden.
Vision is no more—
I am blind.

I have forgotten
(or I never knew)
the inside and outside of words.
Knowledge is, after all, poignant—

Friends, what does
fucking right off
mean to you?

The Madman's War (1974)

This book being poems, how I spent my Canada Council Grant in Mexico and other adventures since that time.

This book is finally dedicated to my mother.

Bar La Cueva

I live in a heat wave and
my eyes sometimes ache
from this new concept
of hot blue.

They cook
shrimp on cement
in the noon day sun.
Shimmering blue.

At high tide
the ocean is coolest.

"us the sea received."

If you believe this
you'll believe anything.

San Blas, Mexico
1968

Tequila Puro

I'm drunk again.
Just a few beers did it
and I'm operating
on yesterday's exhaus-
tion.

Blue again, waiting for
a newscast from California—
it never came.

There is a storm brewing
according to my palm tree
oracular knowledge.
The radio interference
has strengthened my belief.

And over, across the bay,
the lighthouse, the plaintive
horn I sing harmony with.

Of course.

San Blas, Mexico
1968

Another Day in the Bar La Cueva

"Screw art it's an asshole's trade."
Satie

There is a boy,
with intelligent eyes—beautiful with fear.

He can't talk
but aspires to understand.

That's sad.

He sleeps where he falls.

I am fond of silence
and for a few pesos he will smile.

Also, he is an epileptic.

San Blas, Mexico
1968

The Ghost of a Rooster Killed by Ritual

Dead—really got it—was launched
into lonely paradise.

I hung little bells about
to keep off demons;
put flowers in the refrigerator.

I worship my electric fan.

During a storm the Rooster's
ghost got blown away. Out, west,
to sea. He's just vapor you know.

Perhaps he be blown all the
way to Japan or India.

They know what to do with ghosts there.

San Blas, Mexico
1968

King Billy, the Disenchanted

"You may of my glory and my state depose.
but not my griefs; still am I king of those."

            as great as grief the nighttime
spirits give way to the sun.

I remember night, remember the moon—
not modest—brightly down
the cobblestone street gleaming
superstitious light.

            along such streets we take
the air. No soul stirs
except in certain
peculiar shadows
only we seem aware of
and admit.

            Mexico
            1968

Recollection of Celebration

So see I for saying saw;
cloudy in mind,
cloudy in fact in day;
even stormy
earlier when exactly
dawn should have—
then was the wind
insistent, ineluctable and strong
in the coco palms.

Flash, I'm trying to learn
chicken talk.
I will celebrate any purpose
fickle or otherwise.

So say anything with your tears
that you see with your eyes
thereby contribute to decreasing lies.

Somewhere in Mexico
10.10.68

October 1st 1968

a catamite
Mexican tenor
singing tartly.

There are three
tributaries
out of Hell.

He knows all three well.

Puerto Vallarta, Mexico
1968

Male/fail Tale

One last poem
for the lady—

she tried
to be perfect in her way.

One last poem
for the gentleman
who made a perfect getaway.

San Blas, Mexico
October, 1968

Mexican Ice Cream Master

"Women are not made
for farewells," he said
as he pissed.

Before dawn he had begun
the process, churning and blending,
plurals of ingredients.

Taste excellence varies
with effort
and his eyes suggest
his is a competitive field.

Sauta, Mexico
1968

Cerveza Superior

Once, Witch said,
she lived by the sea
or that
it lived by her
and there she ate men raw.

I think Witch is
putting me on in this regard.

I have been accused, by
Witch, of course, of being
affected, of being too much
in the vogue, too full
of gutter dishevelment.

I am content to merely hope
her heart stops soon.

San Blas, Mexico
1968

A Walk In A Certain Plaza

An intersection, firstly,
looking into the Plaza,
eyes open, watching for Federales:
none. Looking again for breast and thighs,
trying to work like a zoom
lens. One antique set only.

From the church steeple
the bell becomes rung
and being ringed
by a boy
with awesome rhythmic
precision.

The baleful bastard.

If I had a bell to ring
or another song to sing?

San Blas, Mexico
1969

A Blue Bell

The plaza is a continuation

If I had a bell to ring
or another song to sing.

Yesterday I met
what was acknowledged
as a happy man.

Today
he died
of carbon monoxide poisoning.

He was just grabbing a siesta
in his garage
prone under a running car
with a broken muffler,

at dawn
in a pool of vomit
leaving two empty mescal bottles

his friends say.

Poopsie/Power/Poem

"I am a lie who tells the truth."
Jean Cocteau

I know nothing of love, there's nothing to know,
You never see it coming, nor see it go.

I held an unconnected
telephone in my hands and tried
to call someone re-assuring; the
telephone was blue
and you were naked.

I trembled inside you, five times,
and then ran out into the street
seeking more of the salvation
I just left.

Today I am left with struggle,
trying to create
a new myth for males.

Batting Practice

It has been a long time,
Madam, long locked in
space—high, outside,
away from you
kind of thing.

A real throw-away
disposable involvement
we have here.

Two balls,
three strikes—
never swing
on a high outside curve ball.

You're out.

Kearney, Ont.
September, 1973

Forslack and Forless

I ran like water, as river might run,
like, like baby to mother—
Jacob's ladder slowly rung by rung.

I ran over desert, got granular in space,
or, or trapped in an hourglass—
I am not fallen! I jumped from grace.

Fucking Ottawa
13.3.74

Rhyme Suggestion

for Therin

You bastard!
Sired by a bastard.
Soon whoremaster to become.
How's every little bit
of every part of you
my good old son.

Eggsucker!
Motherfucker!
Cultural swine.
It pains my arse
to be stuck with a farce
like you as a friend of mine.

Kearney, Ont.
1973

When I Fall In Love

I don't even have to try,
try to understand all this.

Deborah, before we arrived it started.
Everything fell right out.

I used to have a pocket carried love in—
but your music tore a hole in it.

Did you ever swallow a piccolo?
Have elves hid in your hair?

Touching with you was a new feeling.

Toronto
30.7.69

Intimations of Amorality

Hi there, stoned spirit of the flesh.
May I come amongst you?
Would you care to writhe and mesh?

Angel, second order, beloved of god,
To do the boogie is not outlawed.

Magic is what magic does
and that's the truth and it always was.

Kearney, Ont.
1974

The Madman's War

I long to be a carnal scholar!
to essay intimate body details.
I long to speak magic words,
to throw them at some lady's head!

I long to be a war correspondent!
to interview deranged patriots
in some slight nonserious conflict.

If it were credible I would enlist
all the demons Hell hath known
and Frank Sinatra too.

I remain, yours truly,
Zachary Curveball, Lieutenant Commander,
Space Cadets, somewhere
on the North American Front.

The Madman's War: the winter offensive 1973/74

there was a lullaby in the fighting.

I went for a ride in the woods.
I fell off my horse.
I hurt my knee and got violent
with my horse.

My horse ran away and I was still angry.

Casualties were heavy—
I lost my whole fucking army
in the snow.

Currently I am employed as a lumberjack.
Hostilities must cease until
summer warms this old warrior's bones.
Also I am needing a new horse.

A firm steed is what I need.

Declaration of Dependence

I HAVE LOST MY SMALL WAR WITH GOD STOP I WRITE THIS SO AS TO SUE FOR PEACE STOP KNOWING UNCONDITIONAL SURRENDER THE ONLY TERMS AVAILABLE STOP I ACCEPT STOP

SEND COLLECT

Suicide Note

feeling old, knowing
it is happening;

beginning to miss that
foolish boy I was upon
a time once.

Getting curious,
perhaps insane, about
the curve, the corner—
around the bend.

My life has had
sordid details;
real associations
with things obvious,
dark and wrong.

Perhaps I do not believe
in God—but I entertained
great expectations.

And hopes, hopes nourished
by many contradictions.

Somebody has been cutting
the quality of life.

Anonymous

Sweet & Sour Nothings (1980)

for Constance

I

I see an adjectival world.
And I consider all
nouns improper.

In freezing rain—
in March—
in a cold place
filled with diffident people.

There is no antonym for freezing rain I recognize.

2

Seeing Eagles in the dark—
pathetic hallucinations
suffered by one
out of every three.

One out of three.

Trinity is what is sought—
ill deserved and poorly defined.

One out of three
does not play
with a full deck.

3

The mean people, the
spiteful, living from extreme to extreme,
searching for something, or one,
to hurt;
searching to continue their
prevalent pain.

These people surround us.

You surround us.

4

The dark darks, the dark fine hairs,
on the small of your back:
become lighter and lighter as they rise up …
Or the waist—
so small.

These treasures
I have hoarded—
within my mind.

Perhaps to be buried in deep,
yet-to-be-defined
principles.

(In some facetious cases
bottled)

5

The walk, the movement
across the room;

the style of the walk
& the look in the eyes
defines the differences.

However, I have my lust
to keep me going.

6

She moves with a dignity
inspired by fear.
She is beautiful—
she knows it,
& yet she needs something more.

Little Flower I have
lost my faith
in poetry—
in the *veritas* of it all.

But Happy Birthday Baby,
although you may be in the arms of someone new,
I know no thing better than the beauty
I see in you.

7

Ah! existential.

Silence is favoured
in this estate.

As quiet as the sixty-cycle,
as the deaf,
the dead whippoorwill.

8

A Dream

I see a grand procession—these
are dead poets before me—here too
are the dabblers—
am I destined to
be here?

I see a procession
of Protestant Princes
on the final
march past.
An opulent House of Orange—
oil & diamonds—
heads all held high,
ready, even eager, to die,
for a near-forgotten cause:
committed—still they pause …

9

Little Flower, how the world
has made thee:
all the pain, cruelty
I see
will fall from you
as will the petals
of outward annual Beauty.

I will keep you within.
You shall not change.

I will abolish sin.

10

I can give you nothing—
not even advice
& surely not money.

My only gift is one
of questionable genes
& obvious examples
not to be followed.

I have lost control
in a mad world.
Don't follow me looking for happiness.
Love you.

II

I am beginning to understand,
I am learning the lessons,
those ones so hard to learn:
the realities of the ladies;
basic treacherous sweetness, generally;
and men so filled with
greed and violence …

And we are a disgrace.
A "common disgrace."

I have to take my share.

12

On his Thirty-Ninth Birthday

In the midst of the Tulip Festival—
the Festival of Spring—
happens annually where I am—
as leaves and "chervil" sprout—
the natives take to the streets
and hug and kiss
as they walk the byways no longer cold and sinister—
and I celebrate my jackbenny birthday.

Finding that I have less and less to say
and wishing that I could pray:
"Lord send my roots rain."
And please, no more useless pain.

13

I love you
& as I construct
the details of this delusion
the past rolls back on me.

Delusions, I guess,
can be real—
as your body
is real—
& stuns me.

You are a beautiful
concept.

14

I See the Old Chelsea Steeple

In time, I see it, before this highway
was, or I was,
I see it in nineteen hundred & sixty-one—
both so full of life
we held hands with death.

I see it, the Old Chelsea Steeple,
underneath it Dogans pray,
I see it, the Old Chelsea Steeple,
& it marks my Protestant way—

to my home outside of time,
to a life no longer mine.

15

Marvelling at the jive
rolling down the main streets,
down the main line,
as I collect garbage in my taxi
while looking for the disposal area.

And am frankly discouraged, daily,
and manifestly confused
by the human condition.
"That'll be three dollars, baby."

16

Say you love me.
Even lie.

You move, hesitant,
across a room made barren
by your presence.

Later, in 3/4 time,
we shall waltz away to our puerile pleasures
(I do so pray).

17

Once, O how I remember, I was
nearly bejewelled:
lapis & gold.

And, too, I wore the Tetragrammaton,
worshipping the One
on those sexy surrounding streets—
while tomorrow never came.

Now the jewels & gold are gone—
the Tetragrammaton vanished;
however, my lost symbols still
inform me:
tomorrow is just around the corner
of my fuliginous mind.

18

the cigarette saw
the lighter before she—
but he lit it:

he said
"everybody loses,"
as she lit the filter end.

19

They All Love Losers

At twelve, she still
played with dolls.

At eighteen
a NYC abortion
produced real tears.

Inside she's still
wondering
who he was,
where he went
and why she should still care.

20

Gurdjieff Remembered

Active Tense:

She came all over
the room—was
filling space with her pretty.

Passive Tense:

She left—floating through
the room—withdrew, her
and all her pretty, shedding clothes
right down …

Neutral Tense:

I write this and observe
a softened position
on reality.

21

Amongst Mad Dogs

It is difficult to face it/
you have gone a long way
from what you used to be,
from what was
where you were.

Never again,
in my life,
will I leave a forwarding address.

22

And he tried but, too tired to
restore, to rebuild the righteousness
once again in his crippled life,
he manages to walk the streets
of Ottawa just for
diversion.

Or from the corner of Gordon St.
& Fifth Ave., currently awaits
Salvation. And solicits, & hopes
for conversation.

His income: One-hundred and sixty dollars
per month;
this man of all seasons,
this democratic casualty.

23

for Mrs. F.S. Horsey

I have lost so much, Mother
& little of it was mine.

Some pain, yes, lots of pleasure.

And yet I am not a happy man,
but I am getting by & know I always can.

I guess life's strange for us all.
Hang around, take it easy and hope for a windfall.
& I would like to add
that last word
is strange.

24

She/He return from the
lonely place again.

Now he's a fruitarian & eater of bird seed,
even knowing that final
happiness is fugacious.

"Oh Sweetheart if you talk in your sleep,
Don't mention my name,"
my father used to sing.

Let our minds fulminate
and perhaps find agreement.
Perhaps recognize the disasters
we've perpetuated
in pursuit of pleasures we call ideals,
etc.

25

Up the Orange Lodge

And I still see that fat drunk,
the white horse staggering, the
banners flying, my namesake
King William of Orange—
symbolic as hellfire,
as he went to war
to end the Catholic menace,
an annual effort
to drive the Dogans back to Rome.

And I can still smell that summer day.
And can still see my grandfather, another
tragic William, and I, seven or eight,
wondered about Catholics.

Now I, Orange William, find the game beginning to wear
and in my Protestant wisdom simply do not care
as long as they don't shoot me on the street.
Mind you, there are not many I seem to meet.

26

The Lawns of Alta Vista

Dried out & gone hard
with the perception of change; yet
advertised as lush
some sixteen years
in this brain.

I have been dying
on, and along,
with you, your young girls—
with your manicured
green surface, Alta Vista.

Your future?
How about Astro-turf?

27

No more do the chimes tinkle,
or at any rate,
I cannot hear them.

No more do love's bells bong,
not in my head,
I cannot hear them.

And I never have
listened to birds.

I cannot hear them.

28

You

Sometimes, when I'm thinking
I've seen it all,
that life has nothing new
to offer—
I think of you.

Or I think of the images of beauty,
ever changing,
but always, for me, to be found
within you.

Or my thoughts of you …
have I invented this?

29

It's Over

What can I say?
It's over, you can't win?
It's over, & O I remember Roy
Orbison—
& yet it is not. Not quite
like that.

No one should let
beauty perish.
You are a beautiful thing.
We'll think of something
not too bad
we can call me.

30

Canadians Are Good at:

1. Snow Removal.
2. Drinking beer.
3. Going to Florida.
4. Being the voice of reason in a confused world.
5. International simulated boogie-woogie.
6. Collecting Gold Bond Stamps.
7. Newsprint.
8. Shooting hockey pucks.
9.

31

I won't cry so much
tomorrow—
I know too much about drugs
for that.

I won't die so much
tomorrow—
I know too much about thought
for that.

However, you may feel bad
tomorrow—
and will end up pretty sad
about that.

32

You say it's closing in;
there's no room to move—
& your brain is burning.

Well, I haven't truly moved
since 1961;
I am alive
& in my way losing.
But I'm alright.

Getting to the point
where I don't care
where the horses finish—
not wrong but still losing.

To win you must *believe*.

33

As a carpenter or electrician
a man is influenced by his tools.
I hate this pen
& now dislike you.

But I am not a "cynical man"
as you say—
& the pen and you I will never use again.
This observation I suppose one
could call a consolation prize.

34

Much like an early morning moon,
with the sun up,
& you astrally pale.

This place pervades and pulses.

Mister King & his little doggie
walked well-marked paths
& he was tardy, I am told,
in paying his bills.

Gentlemen must know how to lie.
Mister King's kingdom of Canada
was enmeshed in a plural King,
so he, King, was subject to a Kingwe.

William Lyon Mackenzie King
was different & someday
somebody will know.

35

You can hate yourself for loving—
after all it often hurts.
You can hate yourself for not trying—
after all you always end up crying.
That's the way it seems to work,
that's the way it seems to work.

When you're old and feeling finished
and cannot get up for the day,
your soul has somehow been diminished
and you wonder how much more you have to pay.
That's the way it works,
that's the way it works.

Dancing Alone: Selected Poems (2005)

for my mother, always …

Sunrise

for Carl Andries Hamann

Day break me a day of no regret
Regret is the name of the days I get
Day break me this day for I've not lived yet
                    Cuz
                      O
                  I would bring
          lollipops to all bad sad boys and girls
          and would make the livid churches run
          leap frog! leap frog! leap frog!

If you
Sun
   would just break regretless
   with a sunrise of elephant parades
I could bring an end to the reign of trees that bleed
Day break me a day of no regret
Day break me this day for I've not lived yet
Sunrise of elephant parades.

Wystan Hugh Auden

Wystan Hugh Auden
Wrote verse quite sodden.
I knew that he would come to grief
And end up lying for relief.

Wystan Hugh Auden
Was one of the downtrodden
Older boys who persevere
By getting duller every year.

They're the ones who win the prizes
Presenting sheep in multi-guises.
But then if pressed they will confide
Yes, a lion does have pride.

Good bye, good bye, you older boys
Take your rhymes and other toys
So long Auden I'll be like you soon—
Age makes us all our own buffoon.

O Carole

O Carole, Chuck Berry
should have met you,
with yr short hair,
hard eyes & small
soft & suspicious breasts.

O Carole, when did the
milk of human kindness
go sour & yr lips turn
sneeringly down
bitter with loss?

O Carole, the train is leaving the
station full of sensual blacks
chanting choc-o-late!
choc-o-late!

O Carole, keep the faith.
I am the Tooth Fairy's Agent.

Scarlet Woman With Blue Angora Scarf

Well, she knew
how to boogie
and needed a bath.

Although the stars
were right, the Master Therion's
syringe blocked.

And so she waited,
her bright robes fading
& her need to bathe increasing.

In the rocky landscape
of her mind
there is no water,
no greenery
& little hope.

Untitled Fragment

They wonder why he's so cynical,
this man who bottomed out at the pinnacle
of a rather personal success.
You had to give it to him, he tried his best.

He tried for a piece of everything.
He tried to write, he tried to sing.
But it was in the cards: he had to take a fall;
& so he did and later said it didn't hurt at all.

Sacrifice

The blade's sharpness
is clean—on another astral plane
it would have laser potential—
and it seeks soft flesh. An
immaculate incision.

I cannot offer my own skin
to this altar—
and I wonder, dear,
where you are tonight.

How the Dead Prey Upon You

for Ottawa

You and yr past, & re-incarnation, of
all things,
giving you mysterious & yet specious
rights of ownership to a long
catalogue of disgraces
& circuitous lies.

Why not refute the past
and struggle into the future?
You won't have to mix—
stay inside, it is all on TV—
edited for family viewing.
And just like heroin
about five percent real.

Small Ankles, Take Two

Somewhere there
is a girl with small ankles
and I know she waits for me.

She will be refined, this lady,
and delicate—
she will speak in tongues
in the language of The Beast.

Within my recycled mind
I hear strange music.
A dirge, a slow march or processional
to mark her arrival.

I seek ecstasy anticipating
that event.

Dim Aspirations

By candlelight he could pass
as handsome, almost young
& certainly ready;
when the moon breaks free,
bouncing off the snow
he smiles
with his eyes & ears only.

Turning Things Around

for Jody White

Everything in my life is broken—
not smashed nor pulverized—
merely chipped, parts worn away by attrition.
I walk aimlessly to & fro examining
the fragments.
Just so as tonight,
I know, behind that cloud cover
the moon's capabilities broaden.
And I know that Demon well—
as he is mine,
as I am his.

Switching Lanes

for Barbara

Is sanity purpose? Or is
it required, Lady,
in your blonde life?

I look upon the Daisies
you bought—they
stand in a vase beside me,
accompanied by a rose.

I am sure those flowers could talk,
could tell us something.

Unfortunately we killed them,
you and I,
for a smile.

Sheila Frances Louise

I keep my divorce papers
with my underwear, top drawer, in fact,
so that each morning while dressing,
I resolve again,
to stop following my prick around.

No offence now …

Sunrise: Villanelle

for Andries (Maestro) Hamann

Day break me a day of no regret.
Make slow or stop the flow of fear of years.
Day break me this day for I've not loved yet.

Can't we as boys and girls—just islands—
Have no great griefs in our brains and time.
Day break me a day of no regret.

Gladsad street child wanting to hang loose.
Needing a child of morning to love and lose.
Day break me this day for I've not loved yet.

I say sing our songs till our songs send us down.
Where we can lay and listen—hear new sounds.
Day break me a day of no regret.

And that's jazz, you sweet old mother of mine.
High-rolling son of stone-empty pockets.
Day break me this day for I've not loved yet.

And go, planets! go on and twist about,
Children die. Mothers cry. None know why.
Day break me this day of no regret.
Day break me this day for I've not loved yet.

the black prince of bank street (2007)

A Pimping Analogy

Donna was a cocksucker
Working the street
Out Hintonburg way
Until she saw the light. And,
By God, the light was bright!
It flashed, heading east to west,
Almost atomic in it's glare,
So startling to Donna.
She did declare, I've had it—
I'm out of here.
She walks the streets
For Jesus now
And Jesus loves her
Don't you know!

Not Here, Not There

I don't know why there's no love in my life,
She said, her arms outstretched querulous,
But pleading.

I don't mean sex, but it all seems
So far away, so very far away.

I just can't get there.

King Kong Goes To The Shawville Fair

O I went to the Shawville Fair
Hoping to find other Beasties there.
Alas there were none!
But still I had fun
Getting drunk with raccoons
On stale beer.

Constance Maureen

Thing of beauty
Nothing is forever,
I've seen so much sizzle fade,
But my love for you will never
Be enticed to degrade
Until forever is nothing,
And beauty a thing

The End Of The Line

Being drunk, looking down the track,
Waiting for the big train,
Muttering about
An absence of light.

Being sober, looking down the track,
Waiting for the big train,
Wondering why
It's suddenly so bright.

Can I Have This Dance?

So soft of skin, yet harsh of voice—we so
Trapped by the poverty of our aspirations
And capabilities. Limited by our
Loveless dance. Going round
The empty dance floor
One more time.

Do you love me?
(I can barely move)
Do you love me?
(Now I've lost my groove)
Do you love?
(Now that I can't dance)

Maybe Somebody Will Email

Maybe somebody will email
A lonely old man
Who remembers what he wants
And forgets what he can.

Or some sweet thing from the past
Will call & recall things too good to last.
A day of sunshine, full of love,
Ending with dark clouds roiling above.

Birthday Poem

I used to be a star
And when I came out at night
Folks would gather round
And say, my God his light is bright.

But then my light faded
And things are not the same
When I come out at night
They say, what the fuck's his name.

Elegy For Everybody

How strange this growing attachment
To minor keys, or a lonely dog's forlorn
Howling in the prison of a yard;
You can try not to hear it, but then you start to feel it
Echoing in the winter street.

How wonderful is the sunshine
When observed from the shade …
Or seen from the cool dark
Of a personal cave.

Blues Shuffle

We're all old men now,
Have become what we professed to hate,
Wheezing our way, searching out
Those mythical bargains
For unavailable dollars.

Downhill Fleeting

My poor old son, what have you done?
Gone all large, losing
The youthful exuberance,
Encumbered by curses real &
Genetic. Surrounded by mountains
Of snow. Nowhere to go but down,
Down those slippery slopes. Can I come too?

The Return

I saw you in a dream, &
You as real as twenty year ago
Except the hair, not corn-yellow
But black. Warm eyes
Gone cold. But, hey, as the song say,
Got that old feeling, and am going
To run with it.

I can almost feel the soft hair
As it falls through my fingers …

Another Day

for Marilyn

Nearly, no let us say every
Day when I think of you,
Hoping you stay well,
For you enclose my old
Man love/lust in your shoulders, in your arms;
As Jesus said if lustily looking
You become, commit & remain, as
I am, adulterously yours
Darling girl.

I'll see you in my schemes.

Thinking of Cobwebs

for Nelson Ball

When they came they were huge,
Spinning crazily downward—large
Like a giant's hand—
Grabbing folks
And calling them spiders.

Snowflakes, snowflakes,
Evil mutants
That are inclined to melt.

Uncollected Poems (1962-2013)

Zaap

I am a boy
Going door to door
In Ottawa capital of Canada
Advocating nayness
And complete neverness
Singing: B-o B-o B-o
Hold it, lady,
Don't let go

Allen Ginsberg died here
After children read his poems
To a packed house of
Masturbating monkeys
Who sang
B-o B-o B-o
If we can't come
We'll go

Rubber Boots: Canto 1

Pay toilets are driving me
to the woods
(my woods)
But I don't want nails
(jaysus)
or nickels
hate rhymes
and minor poets
tho I never met one
and mostly
lachrymose professors
I am hating
I must insist now
that
I can resurrect the dead
if I want
but they must not die of cancer
no, not cancer
cuz I can't fix cancer
and everyone dies of cancer
more or less
But green babies
are
in
my woods
my own
true
woods
Out! Out!
lousy green babies

Suburban Sublimation

I'm mad!
I'm feeling real mad!
I feel vicious!
Purely vicious!
I feel like slaughtering!
        I think I'll go cut grass.

Val Tetreau Prison

Walls of dragons and birds of prey
Your solidity does not frighten me
Imitation Christ of lightbulbs
You know nothing of the methodist minister
Praying up a storm
Here to visit me in this gloom of cartheft & rape & arson
Bringing a secret plot of escape
Ah minister will we truly walk from here hand in hand
Out onto a lonely pilgrimage to Christ
Will your Buick be big enough to carry me and all my sorrow too
There will surely not be room for all of us and your Bible

Hear me Val Tetreau!
Your maximum security will not help you!
Your Christ of electricity yawns and belches!
Your dragons snap at their chains and care not about me!

Oh Val Tetreau
What use will your evil powers be
When I lead God's warning Angels here
And smash open a void
In which all your black flowers of oblivion
Will be mashed and digested!

Tallahassee Vision & Prayer

for John Stewart Lillico who could not learn either

> You will tell me that you have just learned love;
> I will tell you that you have just learned hope.
>
> William Faulkner, *Light in August*

Dream the easy rule of night upon you & upon this
land of many sorrows & so few dreams,
And bones of new brides swinging lustful from all
 horizon ends,
So nicely new and hopeful.

And then that glorious morning of ravens,
Pitted against the sun—swarming to glory!
And the final mountain, before all who will believe,
Ringed below its crest by the final trees:
Sentinels all for madness.

Can we not, this final & glorious morning,
Ignore the ruined cities, the plagues & sores &
 ugliness of our ravaged bodies, forget the night
 for ever & drink again from beauty—once again
 & finally a deathless lyric issuing triumphant from
 a blind poet's mouth—
And climb towards the sun?

King Kong meets Allen Ginsberg

"Allen, Allen the Universe is tired of me!
"I've seen it in dreams—& me so young!
"All finished my cosmic games."

"Love your mother," he said,
"it doesn't matter,
"God will come."

Hiding in the University's holly bushes,
My fear the reason, I said:
"That bush hurt me!
"I don't understand about love!
"What about cops?"

"Love it, it won't hurt your anymore,
very much.
"Cops are no more
"Love them.
"Don't hurt people."

I left him then
Preaching love to the holly leaves—
Who, bristling,
Waited patiently his first embrace.

Hello

Mother, I would sing you songs
better, much,
than your pills—

& in my song reveries
no one falls down
doped
in a simple bathroom.

The Dance of the Tribe

for Rolf Cahn

The maxim is
be ugly & avoid temptation
& the movement is ugly
& relates only unto itself
nothing more

Among the rushes where the frogs are

their campfires blaze
but give no heat—
all heat is in the dance,
in the shuffle,
the twists & grotesque movements

Among the bulrushes

the chant of the dance
lacks verbs & meanings;
enclitic sounds
with no roots
they drone

where the frogs

& I have seen the catalogues of this death.
this dance of death,
have felt the hand—
seen it go forth
& beckon, beckon …

Are

& the weeping of the people,
for they do weep,
is harmonic,
is appearance here,
here were no thing thrives

the frogs still

it is contained,
careful, seldom flamboyant

among the rushes where they were?

Maryjane

1

Purchase the fire! Yes
buy it from the man,
          the man who has it,
          wants to sell it.

Buy it & use it
                    if you can.

But don't send any to me, please.
          I've got two sticks
                    two sticks
                    two sticks
& one of them is getting hot.

2

In the circle the idea
In the idea the man
In the man many circles
O people what will I do with your circles?

3

The other night one man asked me
why pot? why smoke
that stuff?
            I said
            it helps you to see angels
            if there are any about.
What if
he said
there are no angels
                                        Well
                                        you have fun
                                        looking, I said,
waving goodbye
                        home I was going
                        to see my son
& tell him all about my adventures amongst
horses & Blackfeet Indians.

Mysteriensonaten #1

Biber
your thing
I return
grateful

Born in allegory
the one, man,
manifesting the good, del-
ineating the bad

as a tone
evoked, so
rich. a Stainer,
so plaint-
ive. I cannot
rhythm rich,
transpose ideas
to melody

nor make
the birth,
the One, to All
comprehensible

except
that we are
of, or because of,
that event

we are
because …
he was born
allegorically
to All

Mysteriensonaten #4

for Sheila

I have clung
to your lines,
applying terms
to you, your dimensions.

I think of tenderness
& shake, the music
filling me,
the key of G
at a very old
blues, attacking it.

Let`s go out
to my garden,
the evening is fine
& God`s dampness
is on the flowers & green things,
God`s pity falling on us all.

Mysteriensonaten #5

for Chris

Your eyes are full of paint,
dripping out,
running down your cheeks.

What's happening
on the continual
cross, the symbol ...

Where is your symbol
now—in time, in space?

What happens
really, ever changes
in our symbols,
in our painted terms of life?

Mysteriensonaten #6

Q

How do you
contain a rhythm,
hold it to you
trying to become
it, trying to un-
become yourself?

How does it
stop
just as you're
making it?

A

You have contaminated
what was not yours,
what you did not create.

You will become
that thing, you have now,
& shall cease.

Owned by dead
symbols of your
past life.

Mysteriensonaten #8

I wish you to carry death
as you carry life,
with devotion.

Or die
with vengeance,

you cannot
be replaced
nor can I.

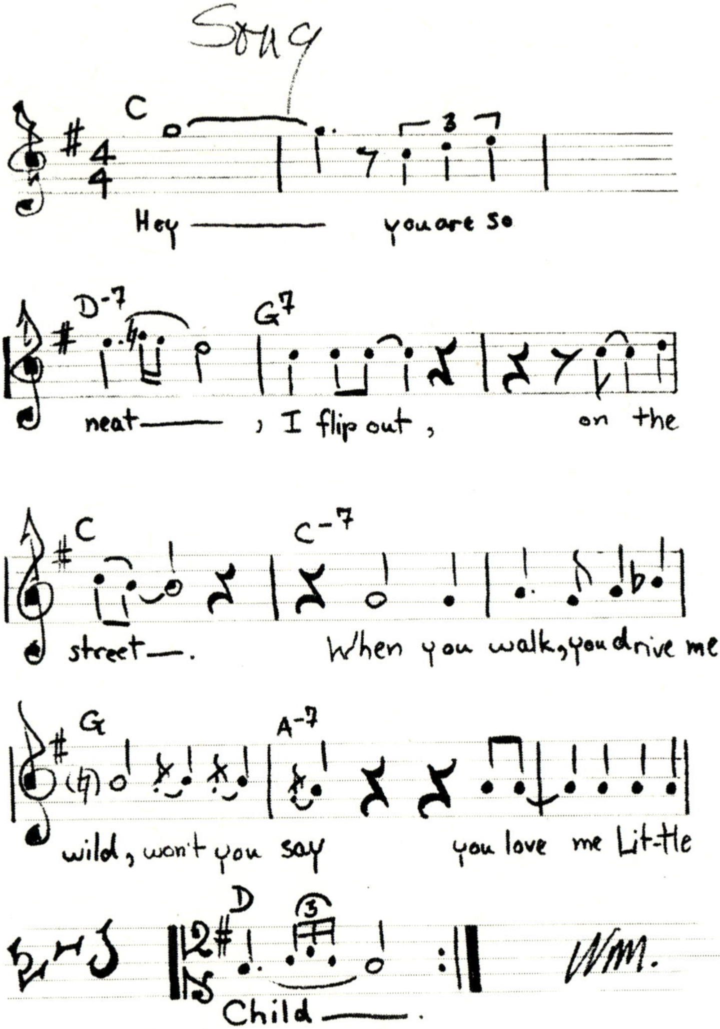
Song
C
Hey —— you are so
D-7 G7
neat——, I flip out, on the
C C-7
street—. When you walk, you drive me
G A-7
wild, won't you say you love me Lit-tle
D
Child——.
Wm.

One Glimpse of a Girl

If it were a rhythm
a vein could contain, or a
quantity,

it is seldom I've seen
more warmth, more hope;

seldom have I loved something
of another gender
as young
as you have become.

In a dark place
my lovely daughter hides
a Spanish boot.

In a dark place, under floorboards,
only she knows—
all the way from Boston
it came, from Spain, to a place
in her thinking heart
of love, a love not fit
for the real world
of smug individuals

& a darkness only a quality boot
could ever occupy.

A Dream

Often a passage, forgotten by logic,
falls open. A break effected by anger gapes
in the space between us.

Finally I realized
that love & the mysteries of touch
operate within & without us both.
I tremble abstractly in separation
as the beam between us wavers,
making new discoveries.

The world must be located, must be
found before lived in. Revered
as sacred.
Our thing lives with a sense profane,
a world of shattered fragments
of blind beliefs, enslaved by mental obligations
to machines.

Here in privileged places
an experience of limitless space
floods our little Universe of lust
& greed. The values & forms you pirouette
for approval become apparent.

Again & again the passage, in flux,
opening & closing; the approaches, the thresholds,
hypnotic sidewalks into strange dream habitations.
Then the numerous rites from a varied &

unfamiliar past, pious ministrations to
gods & spirits who might forbid us
enter. From my mouth such
imprecations scream into
space—a mockery of true prayer,
a chant of fear.

The lonely & only faith in fatal
potential of all things.
Thousands of suns & stars & planets
moving ceaselessly, as if to find
advantageous positions to die in.

Each threshold in the dream
contains answers indicating hope,
a prolonged continuance
of the ride, the lonely journey
on weird breathing vehicles
explained metaphysically as
sacred precincts of eternal soul.

Comic eruptions leap through
the image of an opening—a
communication beyond imagining—
something not belonging
now becomes manifest—incomprehensibly
a sensation of hope
as the dream continues . . .

Provoked by dark night
I imagine a head of mine
on a pillow of granite.

A plan to cancel out tension
succeeds & only slight anxiety
& complete disorientation
are among the recognizable remains
of the mental implosion.

A studied consecration of any space
the whim of night might land in,
the experience of subject
as an illusion of object,
a mammoth silent fellow of the night.

Also in the dream:

An elaborate cannibal cosmos.

Symbols of demons & souls of the dead.

Volumes of discreet but enormous erudition
famous for contradictions.

Spheres overtaken & assimilated
& re-assigned as basic matter
to some as yet untainted corner of space.

Beyond even this crazy fading dream
I see new self-punishing possibilities.

Simple Song

doddle doddle dum
but modal (changes) have not modality.
Music & language cannot contain one another.

I am learning, am beginning to learn,
to be monotonously modal
as I ride out in Notaman Town.

Both sides shuffling
& being strange …
one of the real weird ones

THEY SCORE!

--

the honour of misery
for the plight of others
in pain of others, greater than your own
schadenfreude without malice

not to confuse it
with pity
or emotive poor taste

People suffer because other people
make them suffer, want them to suffer.
I spewed my sensitive egg nog
over India
& am stupid to try
this milkshake
with America in it
to such an intense degree

Sometimes in Quiet Anger

for Dr. & Mrs Schafer

I love in you & in your quiet,
& in your quiet anger   I love thee
for the words you didn't …
O say
can you see the tattered
madman's banner
& the poems of a world
alone in its love
for you?

sometimes in quiet anger,
love, an impartial breeze,
envelopes us
as we try to stand upright
& brings us together as we fall.

Cotton Candy Man

It's sad when all you get is nothing
There's nobody to hold
And you're afraid you're getting old,
And you seem to be losing all the time,
A cotton candy man,
Making all the sweets he can,
But the circus never comes his way.

It's true the ladies have their sweet things
Living in a candy land
And eating on a five-year plan
And their sweets must have constant availability
They don't want a candy man,
Who isn't their ideal old man
A personable also-ran.

Nothing, that's all you get is nothing.
And you're about to blow your mind.
And everybody thinks it's fine
And comments on your becoming immobility,
And you lift your head to shout,
This isn't what life's all about!
This isn't what life's all about!

Gnostic Serenade

And finally we are as the times are,
We meet to part and go diff'rent ways,
And I am trapped on this crazy star,
I've been a pris'ner all of my days.

Once we were young and we laughed a lot,
Happiness wasn't peculiar like today,
But I'd give you everything you think I've got
Just to prove that it needn't be this way.

Yes I know you've found another man,
And yes it was me who left you anyway,
But I'll do anything that I can
Just to convince you to stay.

Don't let the tears start from your eyes,
If you can't make it, I'll find some other way,
Try to be like the stars in the sky,
Just shine on nothing and wait for the end of the day.

Untitled

There really is a secret success to life
Things live that are simply called poems
It appears that the whole thing
is just talking and listening
on a number of levels
I just now referred to them all as
confusing
and I cannot
comprehend it

* * * * * *

I want to write the poem again
I want to hear the song in my ear
I don't really think
I'll ever get what I want, just yet,
But I can't help stop my wanting

Skag Lines

I might move again soon
find something small and open
to do nothing in with pride.

I see that small house
located near the market place;
I know every bar near there.

I'm going to like that small house.

Crowley Visitation

That the actual occult
properties of life
are tied up, if not even
comprised of, absolutely
nothing, has me a little crazy.

How does one live with that kind of preconception
and a dwindling dope supply?

Hey—who is cutting
the qualities of life?

Untitled

Listen, anyone can
read them wrong, them constellations.
Millions of damned
have followed fate blindly
instead of fucking with it a bit.
And only the mad and criminally insane
believe their destiny totally right.

I Came Back

I came back
for the children of the abyss
to become acquainted with

I came back
to testify
on the price of victory
to the big-time losers

I came back
because the game is nearly over
with our whole nut on the line

I came back
to find out
the final score

& here we are
in overtime ...

Still Life

Roses dead;
just two of them …
in an empty wine bottle
they never bloomed fully,
were nipped in the bud by frost,
the blossoms now hang
their dark red heads
showing little passion.

Seem to be asking
for pressing
in some obscure volume
of verse.

Simulated Linguistics

I want to get outside myself,
to observe, directly, simple,
objective things.

I don't want to read
the newspaper,
nor do I need sixty-cycle-
static of any kind.

What I don't want
I don't need.
Yet I need something
and have no name to call it.

The Protestant Prince

His, one of those titles
you inherit—there are
many of them—

arrogant, naughty & stubborn,
bent, battered, yea stoned.

He commands no legions!
In simulated wars he recruits a mob
of men nearly like him
who will fight & die
for nothing. For nothing.
& Jesus wept.

You Can Be Bought

I don't know the exact price;
It could be a dollar
If you're real hungry.

It could be one hundred
If you're easy;
Two hundred and fifty thousand
If you think you're worth a lot—
but out there—on the street
—you can be bought
& if this is just a game …
I hope you don't get caught.

Travels of a Magus

There were so many beaches in the beginning,
so many cold, barren
rocky sea shores—
many would have been discouraged.

And the Scarlet Women,
as they came & went,
took magic away with them.
I wonder did they leave pain?
Was Asmodeus with you?

One novice said:
"Praise God for the mountains:"
as he fell from a precipice
to his startled death
in God's crisp, clean air.

But the Magus moved on,
as did the original Simon,
a brightly glowing spark
in the darkness engulfing what now passes for wisdom
"Do what Thou wilt is the whole of the law."

Cassandra's Xmas Poem

There comes a time, daughter,
when you must face
what preceded thee.

You must look at the poem of life,
understand the rhythm
of your tribe.

But yea be not borne on the winds
called change, by fools (full of feeling: intense).
Nothing changes.
Everything dies.

Miracles occur when or where
neutrality is found
& allowed to perpetuate.

Explanation #3024

I am not a romantic,
not easily swayed by the nicety
of relationships—partings.

Nor a cynic, turned
bitter by an unjust world,
could you call me.

I am nothing—
just like you
on just one more
everlasting Tuesday night.

Surroundings are another matter
both romantically & cynically.
But the operative word
in human affairs
remains hypocrisy
and it has been thus a long,
mighty long time.

I hope this is clear.

Explanation #3025

Please ignore my
previous … even
the noisy sparrows sound good.

It is better I feel
to ignore Rights & Wrongs and
just participate.

The Government, at any rate,
should be pleased.
And one could
get lucky.

King Kong Meets Godzilla

From primordial depths, from God knows what muck,
His hideous form slumbered, or was simply stuck.
As me & mine swung from trees, grabbing fruit
Whilst I grew & grew into a hairy brute.

Was it mankind, in arrogant folly
Caused Godzilla to awake?
As surely as they slotted me into a cage,
Inciting King Kong's murderous rage.

So now we both monsters must hide
In furtive dank places on earth's seamy side,
Where waters do flow but are seldom clean,
And a better life comes only when we dream.

My Next To Last Great Love

apologies to Robt. Browning

There she is, my next to last great love,
Her photo, showing cleavage, wallpaper on my computer screen.
I know now, but could not have earlier foreseen, that dream-
Like quality her eyes contain, her lustrous hair & above
All else the passion she aroused by her glance,
Her heaving bosom & languid sighs held me entranced, & still do,
If the truth is to be told,
As I grow old

Antecedents

As I have trickled out
From a genetic stream of
Purse proud Presbyterians,
Only now falling on dry, hard ground
Among ethnically diverse
Impoverished puritans whose beliefs
Beggar description,
& even comprehension
By the likes of me,

I start to imbibe & little earlier
Each passing day …

March Aubade

Not much of a dawn to sing about, mist punctuated
By rain, shrinking snow showing desperate grass patches;
But the birds are full of song, building nests, or
Whatever. April will be better.

May, the pregnant month, will have me singing
Along with the birds, maybe climbing trees, peering into nests,
Channeling the squirrel within,
The lout without,
Coaxing tulips out of the ground:
An All Canadian pain in the ass.

Memories Memorial

I am old, I am fat
& I am poor & all of that.

But I remember the day.

I have pain to keep me
careful, in these constant,
horrible times.

But I remember the day.

Strobe lights flashing,
beat of the music increasing
as we laughed the time away.

Sure, I remember the day.

With mini skirts,
worn by young flirts,
who danced their blues away.

O yes, fuck oh dear,
I remember those days.

In Memoriam (Sandra Jane Sutcliffe)

Received this photo … you
resplendent in your beauty.
Looking down, a slight smile
beginning at the corners of your
mouth. Beauty never
left you, you glowed defiant,
beyond skin & bone, beyond cancer,
beyond language.

Could never capture you with
mere words & now
you have gone.
You must take my love with you!

Notes on the Poems

Copytext is derived from original book publication of each poem (or periodical appearance and broadside publication in the instance of uncollected poems), unless otherwise noted. Variant texts are indicated.

Shoot Low Sheriff, They're Riding Shetland Ponies!

Self-published by William Hawkins and Roy MacSkimming (Ottawa: [N.P.], 1964). The two decided to publish the book in the wake of the 1963 UBC Summer Poetry Seminar (organized by Warren Tallman featuring Robert Creeley, Robert Duncan, Allen Ginsberg, Denise Levertov, and Charles Olson). MacSkimming and Hawkins had driven to Vancouver from Ottawa to attend. According to MacSkimming, "about 100 copies were printed. The authors sold the book on consignment to booksellers in Toronto and Ottawa for a dollar. In 1965 the remaining stock was turned over to Bill Roberts of Shirley Leishman Books in Ottawa for distribution to the trade" (14). The cover design by Christopher Wells features drawings of Hawkins and MacSkimming printed on orange card stock. The back cover shows a hand giving the finger, with brief bios of each poet underneath. Hawkins's bio reads: "William Hawkins, ex-Ottawa truck driver now drawing unemployment insurance, wrote most of his poems while in various jails."

King Kong Goes to Rotterdam: Originally published in 1962 as a poster poem by Nil Press (Ottawa) designed by Christopher Wells. Roy MacSkimming describes the collaboration between Hawkins and "local artists--the painters Andries Hamann and Christopher Wells, the printer-printmakers Robert Rosewarne and Fran Jones--to create [...] arresting visual settings of his poetry in linocut, printed on big sheets and sold [...] or simply posted around town in busy public places" (11-12). Each poster measures approximately two feet by three feet. An article in the *Ottawa Citizen* from 1962 describes a group of artists, painters and poets printing posters on a "huge 130-year-old 'Washington' Press" (Weiselberger).

This poem was published in *Alphabet* 5 (December 1962) with slight variants in lines two and three: "Why now King Kong me / Me silent seeker of the Rotterdam pussycats / Me troubled watcher of St Orlovsky's bears." The poster poem publication includes the pluralization of "St Orlovsky's bears." It was also republished in *Northern Comfort* (Ottawa: Commoners' Press, 1973) with only the slight variant in line six of "blond" changed to "blonde." See "Untitled (There really is a secret success to life)" in *Uncollected Poems* for a full discussion of *Northern Comfort*.

Postage Stamps: Originally published in 1962 as a poster poem by Nil Press (Ottawa) designed by Robert Rosewarne. In June 1962 the poster poem was reproduced in *Delta* 18.

Two Short Ones: Originally published in 1962 as a poster poem by Nil Press (Ottawa) designed by Robert Rosewarne. It was republished in *The Gift of Space* (Toronto: New Press, 1971) and *Northern Comfort* with a slight variant in the second stanza: lines four and five are collapsed into a single line. *Dancing Alone* (Fredericton: Broken Jaw Press, 2005) restores the original line break.

The Vision of King Mountain: Originally published in *Alphabet* 5 (December 1962). In *Alphabet*, the second stanza is joined to the first, and "automobile-slain" is "automobile slain."

Xochiquetzal: Originally published in *The Canadian Forum* (June 1963) with minor variants. In *The Canadian Forum*, the second line ends with a dash instead of a comma, the third line ends with a colon instead of a comma, "Epithalamium" is given as "Epithalamion" in the fourth line, "top" is not present in the sixth line, the period in line seven is given as a comma, line eight is given as "On your well-seasoned bed.", line nine is given as "Reach with bony hands at the guilt flung pesos as they", the final line ends with an exclamation mark instead of a period, and all "and"s are given as ampersands.

King Kong Goes to Saudi-Arabia: Originally published in *Alphabet* 5 (December 1962). In *Alphabet*, "Chicks" is capitalized in the fourth line. It was republished in *Northern Comfort* with only the slight variant of the first stanza concluding with a dash as opposed to no punctuation. In *Shoot Low* and *Alphabet*, this poem is arranged in two stanzas (the first two stanzas are collapsed into one). In The *Gift of Space, Northern Comfort,* and *Dancing Alone,* it is arranged in three stanzas. This edition takes the later appearances as corrections of the original.

A Song of Flowers: Originally published in 1962 as a poster poem by Nil Press (Ottawa) designed by Christopher Wells.

Porsche: In *Dancing Alone*, "H.G." is identified as Harvey Glatt, longtime Hawkins supporter and patron of Ottawa's music scene through his Treble Clef record stores, concert promotion, CHEZ-FM, and his more recent involvement with True North Records.

Tallahassee: Published in *Delta* 23 (March 1964) with artwork by Christopher Wells. The *Delta* publication includes an epigraph from Gregory Corso's "The American Express": "Hinderov, gentlemen, ever since our arrival, has done what he could to bring insanity and a degree of destruction to man. Bombs, I fully realize, have a drama—they incite, they strengthen and make bold, they grip the imagination—but to what result? Human bodies torn asunder? Devastation with its immutable logic holding final court? Hinderov's victims will not be able to witness the drama, they will be the drama." The *Delta* publication includes several variants: "And tho I do not know you" in the first stanza reads as "Because I do not know you" in *Delta*. There is a dash following "your death history" in *Delta*. Most significantly, there are eight additional lines inserted following the line "for the Sea—":

You Idea
          You Vision
                              You equation of happiness allowed by Time
You Tallahassee
                         I love your doomed name
          & the bricks & rocks & rotten cobs of sooted corn that fly from you
                         cannon
                                   move me not
You, Tallahassee, represent my America
          & to be the ALL of one thing is Horror—
                         then the mar of the whole must be in you.

Billy Graham Goes to Tallahassee: Published in *Delta* 23 (March 1964) as "Billy Graham In Tallahassee" with artwork by Christopher Wells. In *Delta*, "(for he shall rise up from among you)" is not enclosed in parentheses. As well, "his beard full of salt and crabs" is not indented so far over from the left-margin, but is rather placed between the previous and subsequent lines.

Woman from Tallahassee: Published in *Delta* 23 (March 1964) with artwork by Christopher Wells. The *Delta* publication contains substantial variants in the arrangement of the poem on the page, and minor variants in language:

Too bad you are not here with me now
But gone to Tallahassee to work in a coal mine
                    tubercular
                              scraggly-haired
                                        & loving rice
I dream inside your rotting lungs & know
                                                  ultimately
                                        why Tallahassee
                    & wonder if you will be able to get
                              the eyebrow & lash replacements there—
          needed badly if you continue to fight
                                                  the reality of the Sun.

O woman! Heat hording Cracker! That coal will turn to diamonds & blind you! Thunder will come heralding the end of you & Tallahassee too while underneath the crumbling ruins inspired maggots scheme fantastic new things!

The Earth will reverse itself
                              three times
                    & then come water
                                        bringing forth you
                                                            naked
                              with all ugliness washed away
                                                            & all life too

Fire Girl: Published in *Volume 63* 2 (October 1964). In *Volume 63*, the second and third stanzas are condensed into a single stanza.

Louis Riel

Published in *Two Longer Poems: The Seasons of Miss Nicky by Harry Howith & Louis Riel by William Hawkins* (Toronto: Patrician Press, 1965). Copyright note reads: "Louis Riel copyright 1964, 1965 by William Hawkins." An article in *Canadian Literature* 33 (Summer 1967) titled "The Little Presses" by Wynne Francis asserts that Patrician Press was invented by Hawkins and Howith: "Furthermore, a poet often brings out his early books by the simple device of hiring a job-printer and taking care, himself, of the remaining chores of publishing, in which case he sometimes invents a 'press' for the occasion. Thus *Two Longer Poems* by Howith and Hawkins was published by 'Patrician Press'" (61). According to Hawkins, he was "moved by George F.G. Stanley's biography of Riel" and wrote a "36-page sequence of meditations on Riel's visions, madness (the poem's term) and execution" (MacSkimming 14). In the original publication, the individual poems within each part are given on separate pages (as they are in this edition). In *Dancing Alone*, the breaks between sections within each part have been removed, creating a single longer poem within each part. Hawkins also wrote a song with the title "Louis Riel". It can be heard performed by Sneezy Waters on *Dancing Alone: Songs of William Hawkins*.

Part Two: In *Dancing Alone*, "the Count of Cambord" is corrected to "the Count of Chambord." This edition retains this correction.

Hawkins

Published by Nil Press (Ottawa, 1966), subtitled "Poems 1963-1965". The book is dedicated "To "The Children" / at the gate / demanding entrance." The Children was a band that Hawkins was a member of in the 1960s. Nil Press was run by Robert Rosewarne, who had collaborated with Hawkins on the poster poems. The book was distributed by Shirley Leishman Books, as had been the case with some of the copies of *Shoot Low*. The cover features a wrap-around photo of the poet taken by Dr. Edward P. Schafer.

November 17, 1963: Originally published in *Volume 63* 2 (October 1964). In *Volume 63*, the final stanza reads:

But mull over my affairs
real & imagined:
a sad piper for a distant
ridiculous Queen
I court her favour desiring thighs
instead of titles
& see her ass on all my imaginary dollar bills.

Excuses, Excuses: Originally published in *Volume 63* 2 (October 1964) under the title "Of Time & The Aging Girl." In *Volume 63*, there is a comma following the line "rains down harsh words on love" in the third stanza.

Put Down: Originally published in *Volume 63* 2 (October 1964). Also published in *Young Commonwealth Poets '65* (Cardiff: William Heinemann Ltd, 1965). *Young Commonwealth Poets* was produced to coincide with the Commonwealth Arts Festival of 1965 held in Cardiff. Hawkins represented Canada alongside John Robert Colombo, David Cull, Stuart Gilman, James Rother, Steve Smith, David Wevill and Gerald Wilson. Hawkins has two poems in the anthology: "The

Dance of the Tribe" and "Put Down." A notable result of Hawkins's inclusion in the Commonwealth Festival and anthology was that he was honoured as one of Ottawa's "Outstanding Young Men" in 1966. The awards were given "for distinguished service by young men in the community." An article in the *Ottawa Citizen* cites the Commonwealth festival among Hawkins's achievements: "Bill Hawkins, poet and musician, is Canada's own Bob Dylan. He is one of six Canadian literary figures to have been included in the Commonwealth Festival held in Cardiff, Wales, 1965" ("Jaycees honour"). The two other recipients of 1966 were Al Jackson (Ottawa Rough Riders quarterback) and Bill Teron (the town planner responsible for the development of Kanata). The award came with a plaque that "was quickly turned into a cutting board for hash" (Gessell).

The High-Flying Eagle: Originally published in *The Canadian Forum* (September 1965). In *Dancing Alone* the dedication has been expanded to read "for William Roberts." In *The Canadian Forum*, the poem is printed in a single stanza, and the question mark after "Poems" in the second stanza is a period.

Peg's Dream: Originally published in *Alphabet* 9 (November 1964). In *Alphabet*, "house" is not capitalized in the first line.

Autistic: In *Dancing Alone*, lines two and three of stanza one are condensed into a single line, and line three of stanza three is given as "I knew:".

Maidanek: A note in *Hawkins* explains that Maidanek was a Nazi Extermination Camp in Russia.

Four Songs of Experience (I Ching): Originally published in *TISH* 30 (June 1965). Appeared in *New Wave Canada: The New Explosion in Canadian Poetry* edited by Raymond Souster (Toronto: Contact Press, 1966).

There are minor variants in the *TISH* publication; spacing is exaggerated with some stanzas falling further left or right on the page. The only major variant in the *TISH* publication comes in the final stanza of part two. As opposed to reading, "I am indicted / by falling rain," the lines read, "still I am indicated / by falling rain // it is all one." In *New Wave Canada*, the poem appears without its "(I Ching)" subtitle. In *Dancing Alone*, lines one and two of stanza two of part two are collapsed into a single line.

Evidence of Mutations, Changes, etc. (I Ching): Appeared in *New Wave Canada*. In *New Wave Canada*, stanza seven of part one is set on the left margin (not indented as in *Hawkins*), line five of stanza two of part two is joined to line four, and stanza three of part two is broken into two stanzas following line five (these two stanzas are indented). Line two of stanza three of part two is given as "go & give out" and the commas have been removed from the remainder of the poem.

A New Light: Appeared in *Modern Canadian Verse* (Toronto: Oxford University Press, 1967) edited by A.J.M. Smith and *New Wave Canada*. In both of these publications, and in *Dancing Alone*, "For seeing" is not underlined. As well, line five of stanza three is broken into two lines: "it returns / knowing all along."

Letter: Appeared in *New Wave Canada*. In *New Wave Canada*, lines two and three of stanza one are condensed into a single line: "with reality, with words as conveyances." In *The Gift of Space* and *Dancing Alone*, stanza four ends with a period.

Spring Rain: Appeared in *Modern Canadian Verse* and in *New Wave Canada*. In both appearances, lines two and three of stanza two are condensed into a single line. In *New Wave Canada*, the poem ends with an exclamation mark, not a question mark.

For David: Appeared in *New Wave Canada*. Appears as "For David Wiffen" in *The Gift of Space* and *Dancing Alone*. In *New Wave Canada*, lines five and six of stanza two are condensed into a single line.

The Wall: Appeared in *Modern Canadian Verse* and in *New Wave Canada*. In both of these publications, line three of stanza four is given as "predominates."

Schoenberg: Appeared in *New Wave Canada*. The *New Wave Canada* publication includes a variant in stanza one, and an entire additional stanza:

Long-drawn, long-tone out-
side my ear, extended regret
bubbles up & down
& in. The song
lonely, the cry
real as the
mechanism conveying it.

The Krauts
are crying in their ashes
for their geniuses
tonight.

Truth is a convenience
few of us
can afford—
the music is really
everywhere cornering
the day's quota of lies
& will soon be working on tomorrow's.

The Seed: Appeared in *New Wave Canada*.

Mysteriensonaten: The "Mysteriensonaten" poems were published in variously ordered sequences between their initial appearance in *Volume 63* in 1965 and *Dancing Alone* in 2005. In total, nine distinct poems appeared numbered under the title "Mysteriensonaten." What was published as "Mysteriensonaten #3" in *Hawkins* was published as "Mysteriensonaten #10" in *New Wave Canada*, suggesting there is at least one more poem unaccounted for. *Hawkins* (1966) indicated a core group of four poems that perhaps constitute the version of the series that most satisfied the poet. However, these four poems also appeared under different numbers. #1 in *Hawkins* appeared as #6 in *New Wave Canada*, #7 in *Volume 63*, and as the sole remnant of the series, simply "Mysteriensonaten," in *The Gift of Space* and *Dancing Alone*. The four published in *Hawkins* are reprinted in order under *Hawkins* in this collection. The remaining five poems that appeared only in literary journals are printed under *Uncollected Poems* with their periodical numbering intact, despite the fact that this numbering conflicts with the poems from *Hawkins*.

Mysteriensonaten #1: Originally published as "Mysteriensonaten #7" in *Volume 63* 4 (Winter 1965). Appeared in *New Wave Canada* as "Mysteriensonaten #6." Appears as "Mysteriensonaten" in *The Gift of Space*. The final stanza of the poem appeared, without title or reference, in *Minutes of the Last Meeting*, published in 1993 in issue "Six Seven Eight" of *The Outsider* (issued by by jwcurry (Room 302 Books), Nicky Drumbolis (Letters Bookshop) and D.M. Owen (Martin Garth Press).

Mysteriensonaten #3: Appeared in *New Wave Canada* as "Mysteriensonaten #10." In *New Wave Canada*, the question mark at the end of stanza four has been removed.

Mysteriensonaten #4: Appeared in *New Wave Canada* as "Mysteriensonaten #7." In *New Wave Canada*, the first comma in line three is replaced with a dash.

Fragment of a Conversation: Appeared in *New Wave Canada*. In *New Wave Canada*, the poem appears without the dedication "for Elizabeth," but does include a date: "23/5/65." In *The Gift of Space* and *Dancing Alone*, lines three and four of stanza one are condensed into a single line.

Getting Up: A Glimpse of the Poet-Anima in the Nude: In *The Gift of the Space*, the title is given as "Getting Up: A Glimpse of the Poet-Animus in the Nude."

What He's Waiting For: Appeared in *New Wave Canada*. In *New Wave Canada*, lines four and five of stanza one are condensed into a single line.

Ottawa Poems

Published by Nelson Ball's Weed/Flower Press (Kitchener, 1966), reprinted in 1967. Like many other books published by Weed/Flower, *Ottawa Poems* has a cover design by artist Barbara Caruso. A series of overlapping thick black lines look like streets, and two hands offer the only recognizable point of reference.

Ottawa Poems has been through several different iterations in its print history. The version used in this book follows the original Weed/Flower edition. In *The Gift of Space*, *Ottawa Poems* would be trimmed from its original twenty-eight parts to twenty-four. The new twenty-four-part edit was renumbered sequentially, suggesting a new coherent and complete edit. The pieces removed were: "#8 Poem in Red Ink", "#20 The Last Poem for People", "#24 Characterology", and "#26 Almost a Poem." A textual error in *The Gift of Space* sees "#21 Sorry, This Is It" printed in position #19 in the new sequence, yet still numbered #21, only to be followed by a second #21. The William Hawkins Fonds at the University of Calgary contains a revised proof of *The Gift of Space* manuscript. The 39-page document consists of the same selection of poems in the same order. Interestingly, this particular edit of *Ottawa Poems* is given a new title, "Catch Line," with the curious handwritten note "Take 8." As well, the textual error naming two poems #21 is not present; "Sorry, This Is It" is marked as #19. The error must have been introduced at a later stage in the publishing process. In *Dancing Alone*, the original numbers are restored and the poems excised in *The Gift of Space* are left as gaps. A further two poems are removed ("#9 A Stupid Canasta Poem" and "#13") reducing the sequence to twenty-two parts. Four sections from *Ottawa Poems* also appeared in *New Wave Canada* (1966) with further deviations in numbering. "#5" appears as "#7," "#11" appears as "#17," "#13" appears as "#24" and "#16" appears as "#25." Further appearances of these poems in magazines are listed below. The epigraph from Paul Foster Case is not given in *The Gift of Space* or *Dancing Alone*.

#2: In *The Gift of Space*, stanza one ends with a dash, not a comma.

#3: In *The Gift of Space*, the second-to-last line does not include the parentheses given in all other appearances.

#5: Appeared as "#7" in *El Corno Emplumado* 19 (July 1966) coincident with the publication of *Ottawa Poems*. In *El Corno Emplumado*, the first comma in line three is not present, and stanza two ends with a question mark as opposed to an ellipse. *El Corno Emplumado* was published out of Mexico City. This issue featured thirteen Canadian poets (including George Bowering, Fred Wah, John Newlove, Nelson Ball, Daphne Buckle, Red Lane, and others). Also appeared in *New Wave Canada* with same variant in stanza two. Also in *New Wave Canada*, stanza four ends with "crowded busloads" as opposed to "crowded busload." In *The Gift of Space* and *Dancing Alone*, line two of stanza one replaces "capitol?" with "capital?"

#10: In *The Gift of Space*, stanzas two and three are condensed into a single stanza.

#13: Appeared as "#25" in *New Wave Canada*. In *New Wave Canada*, the first comma in line two of stanza two is not present.

#14: In *The Gift of Space* and *Dancing Alone*, the first line of the third stanza is given as "& the kid blows a riff".

#15 "Ah shit don't shoot I'll sing": Republished in *Northern Comfort*. This publication includes several substantial variants:

I sing:

Ottawa
rivers & jails
fantasies

the dawn just can't
slow up.

For song:
I sing
Ottawa
and you know nothing
of song
you're just a poem
you're nothing but
a poem.

I sing:
buses and
actual criminal exhaust
people are falling
victim to their conveniences

the man
vibrated to death
by his electric toothbrush

and me,
hey listen,
I take drugs.

Listen Ottawa, I can't sleep.
seem to have forgotten
the ancient art.

expect maybe too much—
the ancient dawn
is now happening

& it does give me
incentives
but its too late.

Can't you give me one more story?
Get me into one more day.

#16 "Beauty will not wait": The title is a quotation from Charles Olson's "Letter 22." Appeared in *New Wave Canada* as "#25." In *New Wave Canada*, the semi-colon in stanza four is given as a dash.

#23 Hello From The Shadows: Originally published in *Weed* 4 (July/August 1966).

#24 Characterology: Appeared in *IS* one (1966). The poem is not numbered, appearing simply as "Characterology."

#25 The Last Train to Narcissus: Originally published in *Weed* 4 (July/August 1966).

#26 Almost a Poem: Appeared in *Volume 63* 5 (Summer 1966). The poem is not numbered, appearing simply as "Almost a Poem."

#27 Books On Iran Wanted: Originally published in *Weed* 4 (July/August 1966). In *Dancing Alone*, the first line is given as: "or conversations with the hip Persian who says".

The Gift of Space: Selected Poems 1960/1970

Published by New Press (Toronto, 1971). *The Gift of Space*, Hawkins's first selected poems, collected material from *Shoot Low, Hawkins* and *Ottawa Poems*. Nothing was included from *Louis Riel*. Twenty-one new poems were also printed, and represent the only material from *The Gift of Space* reprinted in this volume. Roy MacSkimming was a partner at New Press and was the editor responsible for the selection of work. In his introduction to *Dancing Alone*, MacSkimming writes, "[*The Gift of Space*] drew on what I considered to be Bill's best work [...]" (17). The cover was illustrated by Christopher Wells. Hawkins is portrayed riding on the shoulders of King Kong in front of a landscape of trees. Each tree has a mouth. The back cover shows a small photograph of Hawkins in its centre. The images are black and white on white paper. The colophon indicates that the collection was published simultaneously in hardcover and paperback, but it was only issued in hardcover. The hardcover edition is bound into black cloth, with silver titles and black endpapers.

Wilful Murder: Originally published in *Hyphid* 1 (January 1968). In *Hyphid*, line seven reads: "& word about thorns." Also in Hyphid, line sixteen reads: "The Saint saves his winter snowballs until July." It was republished in *Northern Comfort*.

Mother, the Angel of Death in My Dreams: Originally published in *Weed* 9 (May/June 1967). In *Weed*, the final line of the first stanza reads "half the living time" as opposed to "all the living time" in *The Gift of Space*. There are two other small variants. In the second stanza, the *Weed* publication does not capitalize "Great Enemy," though it is capitalized in *The Gift of Space*. As well, in the third stanza, "reappear" is on the third line, not the second line. In *Dancing Alone*, this poem's title is given as "Angel of Death in My Dreams."

A Poem About Tomorrow: Originally published in *Hyphid* 1 (January 1968).

Before She Could Do It: Originally published in *LUV* 1 (1967). In *LUV*, the final period is not included and "To" is not capitalized at the beginning of the third stanza. The title is given as "Before She could do it."

The Gift of Space: Originally published in *Hyphid* 1 (January 1968).

The Warner Mystique: Originally published in *Hyphid* 1 (January 1968).

Projective Tulips: Originally published in *Hyphid* 1 (January 1968). In Hyphid, the first word of the poem is not capitalized.

Weather Report: Originally published in *Weed* 11 (September/October 1967). In *Weed*, the poem is dated "29/5/67". It appeared under the heading "... from a notebook" with an additional untitled poem (first line: "the honour of misery") included under *Uncollected Poems* in this volume. The two versions contain minor typographical differences in capitalization and punctuation. The second stanza, however, is substantially different. The second stanza of the poem as it appears in *Weed* reads as follows:

cosmic cannibals
are coming
& they are, they are
going to gobble up all death things,
regardless of tradition,
& I'll bet half dead things too

In *Weed*, the third stanza ends without punctuation, whereas it ends with "—:" in *The Gift of Space*.

Σατάr: The revised proof of *The Gift of Space* in the William Hawkins Fonds at the University of Calgary give this title as "Satar." The other Greek word in the first stanza is given as "opxie."

The Madman's War

Published by S.A.W. Publications (Ottawa, 1974). *The Madman's War* was Hawkins's final collection of his most productive period. 300 copies were produced (twenty-eight of which were signed by the poet). Inconsistencies with locations and dates included with poems are original to the book. Hawkins is pictured on both front and back covers in photographs by Peter Lamb. On the front he is shown with a gun nested between his leg and arm. On the back he is shown with his head wrapped in a bandage. Macskimming describes the book's spirit as one of "exhaustion and futility" (17). A useful reference for these poems is a lyric in Hawkins's song "Alison": "I been a year in Mexico and it rearranged my head / the love I have inside of me is much more alive than dead."

Tequila Puro: In *Dancing Alone*, the first stanza is given as: "I'm drunk again. Just a few beers did it / and I'm operating / on yesterday's exhaustion."

King Billy, the Disenchanted: Uncredited epigraph is from William Shakespeare's *Richard II*.

Declaration of Dependence: This edition retains the original line breaks from *The Madman's War*. In *Dancing Alone*, the first stanza is given in three lines:

I HAVE LOST MY SMALL WAR WITH GOD STOP I WRITE
THIS SO AS TO SUE FOR PEACE STOP KNOWING UNCONDITIONAL
SURRENDER THE ONLY TERMS AVAILABLE STOP I ACCEPT STOP

Sweet & Sour Nothings

Published in *Anthos* 2:1&2, a "Special/Double Ottawa Issue" (1980). Following *The Madman's War* in 1974, Hawkins entered a period of extended publishing silence. *Sweet & Sour Nothings* was to be Hawkins's seventh book. An article in the *Ottawa Citizen* discussing a reading series hosted at the University of Ottawa makes this clear: "Bill Hawkins, whose new book, *Sweet and Sour Nothings*, is coming out this year [...]" ("Area poets"). However, the book never appeared. This issue of *Anthos* was dedicated "with love and respect to Williams Hawkins." It also included a photo of Hawkins playing the guitar, an introductory note by Hawkins on David Wiffen, and a review of George Johnston's *Taking a Grip* by Hawkins. Hawkins's biographical note in *Anthos* reads: "He has no biographical statement to make other than: he continues as before—just not smiling, as much, anymore. He has published six books and is currently working on his seventh." This was followed by the publication of the poem "Still Life" as a broadside, also by Anthos Books (see *Uncollected Poems*). In 2010, Apt. 9 Press (Ottawa) published *Sweet & Sour Nothings* for the first time as a discrete book. The text, as it appears here, was edited by Roy MacSkimming for the Apt. 9 edition. The cover of the Apt. 9 edition uses an image derived from Jennifer Huzera's photograph "Tulips." Variants from the *Anthos* text are noted below.

4: In *Anthos*, the second stanza ends with a semi-colon, not a period. Consequently, the first word of stanza three is not capitalized. Also, the second line of stanza four reads: "yet to be defined," without dashes. The poem ends with a period following the parenthesis.

6: In *Anthos*, line two of stanza one ends with a semi-colon, not a period. Consequently, the first word of line three is not capitalized. "Happy Birthday" is not capitalized in the third stanza.

9: In *Anthos*, line two of stanza one ends with a semi-colon, not a colon. As well, stanzas one and two are given as a single stanza.

10: In *Anthos*, this poem is dedicated "for Andries, Jennifer, and Cassandra."

11: In *Anthos*, the semi-colon in line four of stanza one is given as a colon.

14: In *Anthos*, "Protestant" is given as "protestant" in line four of stanza two.

16: In *Anthos*, the period that ends the poem is placed outside of the parenthesis.

17: In *Anthos*, this poem is dedicated "for Patrick and Joanne White." As well, lines two and three of stanza one read: "nearly be-jewelled: / Lapis & gold."

18: In *Anthos*, the final line reads: "as she lite the filter end."

22: In *Anthos*, the first stanza reads:

And he tried, but, too tired to
restore, re-build the righteousness
once again in his crippled life,
he manages to walk the streets
of Ottawa; I guess, just for
diversion.

25: In *Anthos*, "Dogans" is given as "dogans" in line nine of stanza one. Also, line two of stanza three ends with a semi-colon.

26: In *Anthos,* the final line reads: "How about astro turf?"

33: In *Anthos*, the second line of stanza one ends with a colon, not a period. As well, only "cynical" is enclosed in quotation marks in line one of stanza two.

34: In *Anthos*, the final line of stanza three is given as an individual stanza. Also, the fourth stanza reads:

Gentlemen, must know how to lie.
Mister Kind's kingdom of Canada
was enmeshed in a plural King,
so he, King was subject to a Kingwe.

35: In *Anthos,* line three of stanza one does not include the dash.

Dancing Alone: Selected Poems

Published by Broken Jaw Press (Fredericton, 2005). *Dancing Alone* is Hawkins's second selected poems. It was produced as the fifth entry in the rob mclennan-edited Cauldron Books imprint in an edition of 500 copies. mclennan describes its production:

> The story, as I understand it, tells that it was Ottawa gadfly and mystic, Noel Evans, after some slight prodding from Bill, who originally prepared the manuscript around 1996. Once completed, neither of them could find a home for the collection. It was Bill, in 2002, who brought the disk to me, saying something along the lines of, I don't know what to do with the damn thing. You take it.
>
> I spent the next two years searching out other poems of Bill's that might fit into the manuscript, from lost pieces in issues of Nelson Ball's *Weed* or *Canadian Forum*, as the discovery of each new poem excited him until he saw them again, causing him to gruff that under no circumstances should I put "that poem" into the final manuscript. In the end, the book remains what Evans had put together, and no more. ("The Return of William Hawkins")

The cover is an image by Christopher Wells. The book has a Preface by Bruce Cockburn, who declares, "when i started writing songs, it was to put music to Bill Hawkins's lyrics" (9). It also has an extended introduction by Roy MacSkimming which balances personal anecdotes with publishing and professional details. Included are selections from all of Hawkins's previous books (including the entirety of *Louis Riel*), as well as several new poems.

Sunrise: Originally published in *Alphabet* 5 (December 1962). The *Alphabet* publication contains variants in the final ten lines:

If you
Sun
          would just break regretless
   with a sunrise of elephant parades
                              that would keep all turtles safe
                    for a sunrise of elephant parades
 I would bring an end to the reign of trees that bleed
Day break me a day of no regret
Day break me this day for I've not lived yet
Sun   rise   of   elephant   parades.

Untitled Fragment: Originally published in *The Canadian Forum* (June 1993).

How the Dead Prey Upon You: Originally published in *The Canadian Forum* (June 1993). Also published in *ottawater* 1 (January 2005).

Dim Aspirations: Originally published in *The Canadian Forum* (June 1993).

Turning Things Around: Originally published in *The Canadian Forum* (June 1993). In a typescript held by Joanne Wiffen (see "Simulated Linguistics" in *Uncollected Poems* for a full discussion of this typescript), there is an additional line to this poem. Lines seven to nine read: "I know, behind that cloud cover, / the moon's capabilities broaden, / as if filled by a Demon's Eucharist."

Switching Lanes: Originally published in *The Canadian Forum* (June 1993). In *Dancing Alone*, the first word of the poem is not capitalized.

However, it is capitalized in the Wiffen typescript as well as in *The Canadian Forum*. I have capitalized here for the sake of the internal consistency of the poem and in deference to these earlier publications.

Sheila Frances Louise: Originally published as an above/ground press broadside (#206, Ottawa 2004); 500 copies were produced in April-May 2004. Also published in *ottawater* 1 (January 2005).

Sunrise: Villanelle: Originally published in *ottawater* 1 (January 2005).

the black prince of bank street

Published by above/ground press (Ottawa, 2007). It is minimalist in its production (consistent with the above/ground press aesthetic), with only the title and Hawkins's name printed on a clean blue cover with blue endpapers. 300 copies were produced. The full chapbook was reprinted, unchanged, in *Ground Rules: the best of the second decade of above/ground press* (Ottawa: Chaudiere Books, 2013).

King Kong Goes To The Shawville Fair: Originally published in *ottawater* 1 (January 2005). Hawkins's biographical note in *ottawater* states this "is his first new poem since 1990."

Constance Maureen: Originally published in *Peter F. Yacht Club* 4 (May 2005). The poem ends with a period in the *Peter F. Yacht Club* publication.

The End Of The Line: Originally published in *Peter F. Yacht Club* 4 (May 2005).

Elegy for Everybody: Originally published in *ottawater* 3 (January 2007).

The Return: Originally published in *Peter F. Yacht Club* 4 (May 2005).

Another Day: Originally published in *ottawater* 3 (January 2007).

Thinking of Cobwebs: Originally published as 1cent leaflet #362 by jwcurry. Published in an edition of "110 copies as the webbing liquidifies / uncommonly early this 15 march 2005" according to the leaflet.

Zaap: Published as a poster poem in 1962 by Nil Press (Ottawa) designed by Andries Hamann.

Rubber Boots: Canto 1: Published as a poster poem in 1962 by Nil Press. The poster received a review in *Alphabet* 4 (June 1962):

> Also a smart Interior Design grad should think of poetry wallpaper. If the rich won't buy it between covers, perhaps they'd like it on their walls. Rilke for the spare room and Ezra Pound for the counting house. Well, here's your chance! William Hawkins has come forth with a very broad, boldly and brightly designed broadsheet that would do something to any party and any room. Here is a youthful, very natural talent. With his capacity for epigram Mr Hawkins should write a play and I hope he wallpapers a castle.

Suburban Sublimation: Published in *The Canadian Forum* (March 1962). This poem is also printed in an article in the *Ottawa Citizen* ("Of Dadaism, Nietzsche and Zen Buddhism" 20 February 1962).

Val Tetreau Prison: Published in *Evidence* 6 (n.d.; *Evidence* 5 was dated 1962). According to Roy MacSkimming, "Bill had been doing time in Quebec's Val Tetreau correctional institution for some misdemeanor involving other people's cars. He had the tattoo to prove it—a pattern of five bluish-black dots on the back of his left hand, the mark by which alumni of the prison system recognized each other" (11). His biographical note in the issue reads: "WILLIAM HAWKINS was born in Ottawa in 1940 and says that he 'left same as soon as was possible. Travelled, dreamed angels and returned to live in the Gatineau Mountains. Val Tetreau, where I spent the Christmas of 1958, is located 5 miles from my present home.'"

Tallahassee Vision & Prayer: Published in *Something Else* 1 (March 1963). *Something Else* was a short-lived literary magazine edited by William Hawkins and Denis Faulkner. It was designed by Robert Rosewarne, and lists Harry Howith and F.A. Harvey as "Associates." Only one issue was published. *The Canadian Author & Bookman* 38:4 (Summer 1963) describes the magazine: "as yet far from luxurious in presentation, but also commendable in content, ... *Something Else* is a spirited newcomer to the periodical scene ... like many another magazine in Canada, it appears to be functioning not in accordance to the laws of economics, but on faith, hope, and precious little charity. We can only wish it luck and send in our three dollars (for six issues, interval not specified). Address: 248 Bank Street, Ottawa." 248 Bank Street was home to one iteration of the legendary Le Hibou Coffee House (founded by Denis Faulkner). The first and only issue features poetry by Irving Layton, George Johnston, Aaron Greenberg and Peter Bogan. In addition to poetry, the magazine contains articles on Dylan Thomas, the administration of the Nobel Prize in Literature, and a history of the social credit movement. Typographically and aesthetically, it resembles *Shoot Low* and *Harry Howith's Burglar Tools* (Ottawa: Bytown Books, 1963), suggesting the same printer was used. It contains ads for The Treble Clef (owned by Harvey Glatt, longtime Hawkins supporter), the Ottawa Bookhunter ("Out of Print Titles Obtained"), George D. Howith Insurance, a production of "Can Can" at the Ottawa Technical High School, and The Little Blue Barn ("Fine Teak Furniture in Bells Corners"). Hawkins's poem is related to the Tallahassee poems of *Shoot Low*, though it was only published in this issue of *Something Else*. Also included is a short essay by Hawkins on artist Frank Mayrs.

King Kong meets Allen Ginsberg: Published in *Volume* 63 1 (December 1963).

Hello: Published in *Volume* 63 2 (October 1964).

The Dance of the Tribe: Published in *Volume 63* 2 (October 1964). Also published in *Young Commonwealth Poets '65*. See note regarding "Put Down" in *Hawkins* for a further explanation of *Young Commonwealth Poets '65*.

Maryjane: Published in *Volume 63* 2 (October 1964).

Mysteriensonaten #1: Published in *Volume 63* 4 (Winter 1965). See note regarding "Mysteriensonaten" under *Hawkins* for a full discussion of this sequence.

Mysteriensonaten #4: Published in *Volume 63* 4 (Winter 1965).

Mysteriensonaten #5: Published in *Volume 63* 4 (Winter 1965).

Mysteriensonaten #6: Published in *Volume 63* 4 (Winter 1965).

Mysteriensonaten #8: Published in *Volume 63* 4 (Winter 1965).

Song: Published in the "*New Wave Canada* Portfolio" in *Island* 7/8 (1966). The portfolio included reproductions of hand-written poems by fourteen of the contributors to *New Wave Canada*.

One Glimpse of a Girl: Published in 1967 as *PLIEGO-CANADA Broadside XLII* (Portland, Oregon: Wine Press, 1967). Wine Press was run by Carlos Reyes. Nelson Ball edited the Canadian series (numbers 42-48), producing six broadsides in 1967 (also published were Angelika Sommer [twice], David McFadden, Chuck Carlson and Bruce Cockburn). The sheet is single sided (8.5x14"), with "PLIEGO-CANADA" hand stamped and "XLII" hand written.

A Dream: Published in *Weed* 9 (May/June 1967).

Simple Song: Published in *Weed* 9 (May/June 1967).

-- (the honour of misery): Published in *Weed* 11 (September/October 1967). Appeared under the heading "... from a notebook" along with "Weather Report" which would appear in *The Gift of Space*.

Sometimes in Quiet Anger: Published in *Hyphid* 1 (January 1968). Dr. Edward P. Schafer took the photo of Hawkins used on the cover of *Hawkins*. Also printed in this issue: "The Gift of Space," "The Warner Mystique," "Projective Tulips," "Wilful Murder" and "A Poem About Tomorrow," all of which would appear in *The Gift of Space*.

Cotton Candy Man: Published in *Poetry of Relevance* (Toronto: Methuen, 1970). These are song lyrics written by Hawkins and recorded by Three's a Crowd. *Poetry of Relevance* "[invited] students to find significant connections between poems of our literary heritage and songs that express contemporary interests and concerns" (v). Song lyrics, ranging from Joni Mitchell and Pete Seeger to The Beatles and The Doors, were paired with "relevant" poetry. Hawkins's lyrics appear alongside Percy Bysshe Shelley's "Stanzas: Written in Dejection, near Naples," Maria Nunez's "Empty," Michael Drayton's "Farewell to Love," and George Meredith's "Thus Piteously Love Closed What He Begat." Hawkins protégé and frequent collaborator Bruce Cockburn also has lyrics featured. Hawkins biographical note reads:

> Like Bruce Cockburn, William Hawkins, another writer from Ottawa, composes both poetry and songs. His intimate knowledge of the difference between poem and song is reflected in the way he enables his songs to carry poetry richness without overburdening the easy, idiomatic style that is essential to the popular song form.

"Cotton Candy Man" and "Gnostic Serenade" are the only song lyrics included in this volume. Songwriting is collaborative by nature, and Hawkins's songs were primarily recorded by artists other than himself. These conditions create problems determining to whom lyrics should be credited. These two have been included as they were published in print under Hawkins's name in a poetry anthology. Both sets of lyrics were "Used by permission of Bytown Music" in *Poetry of Relevance*.

Gnostic Serenade: Published in *Poetry of Relevance* (Toronto: Methuen, 1970). See note regarding "Cotton Candy Man" in *Uncollected Poems* for a full discussion of *Poetry of Relevance*. The lyrics to "Gnostic Serenade" were also printed in *Sparks: Poetry Newsmagazine* 1:11 (January 1978), though in slightly different form as follows:

And finally we are as the times are
We meet to part and go our separate ways
But I'm trapped on this crazy star
I've been a prisoner all my days
Once we were young and we laughed a lot
Happiness wasn't peculiar like today
But I will give you everything you think I've got
Just to prove it needn't remain this way
Don't let the tears start from your eyes
If you can't make it I'll find another way
Just try to be like the stars up in the skies
And shine down on nothing
Just wait for the end of day.

Untitled (There really is a secret success to life): This poem, and the three that follow, were published in *Northern Comfort* (Ottawa: Commoners' Press, 1973) in an edition of 500 copies. The title page describes the book as follows: "being a reading of poetry by various people, given in the back yard of the Victoria Hotel 18 Murray Street, the Byward Market, Ottawa, on the evening of June 29th, 1972." The text was transcribed from recordings provided by "Peter Lamb of Coon Hollow Films and Mariea Sparks of Ottawa Living Radio." It was transcribed by "Monk Besserer." The list of readers, speakers, and musicians includes William Hawkins, Alyx Jones, Robert Hogg, Marius Kociejowski, Christopher Levenson, Neil Whiteman, Jack Nathanson, George Johnston, Ronnie Judge, "Unknown Reader," David Andrews, The 47 Argyle Street Band, Christopher James and Bill Stevenson. The charm of the book lies in its apparent faith to the recording. The transcription includes the speakers, banter, introductions, comments from the audience, as well as a generous selection of photos of the event. Hawkins, in addition to reading, hosted the evening. Hawkins read from the recently published *The Gift of Space* ("King Kong Goes to Rotterdam," "Two Short Ones," "King Kong Goes to Saudi Arabia," "Wilful Murder," "Ah Shit Don't Shoot I'll Sing"). He also read the four new poems included here. The asterisks that break up the two sections of "Untitled (There really is a secret success to life)" are included in *Northern Comfort*. It is possible that this poem is, in fact, two poems. However, Hawkins declares that he will read "four new poems," a statement that precipitated publishing this as a single poem.

Hawkins biography in the book reads: "William Hawkins, 33, lives in Mexico at 182 ½ Dalhousie Street. In 1967 he was voted one of Ottawa's Finest Young Men." The reference to Mexico touches on the poems he wrote on a Canada Council Grant in the late sixties and early seventies that would be published the following year in *The Madman's War*. The "Finest Young Man" Award was actually an "Outstanding Young Man Award." See note regarding "Put Down" from Hawkins for a full discussion of this award.

Skag Lines: Published in *Northern Comfort*. Hawkins introduces this poem by saying, "Now for any of you that do not know what 'skag' is, that is hip jargon for heroin" (9).

Crowley Visitation: Published in *Northern Comfort*.

Untitled (Listen, any can): Published in *Northern Comfort*. Hawkins introduces this poem by saying, "the first two lines are in Greek, which I'm going to pass over ... the two lines mean, one is ... 'One who contemplates his own death' and the other line is 'One who devotes himself to the study of the constellations'" (9-10).

I Came Back: Published in *Sparks: Poetry Newsmagazine* 1:11 (January 1978) with the note, "This poem, dated April 11, 1976, is previously unpublished." This poem, and the lyrics to "Gnostic Serenade" discussed above, are accompanied by a short interview. The unidentified interviewer writes,

> The poet is tallish, solidly built, with a vague air of being ready for anything. (A fight? A revelation?). He wears a Fu-Manchu moustache and a Depression Era cap with a silver Maple Leaf stuck into it. Present occupation: Taxi driver. A man who works ten hours a day, and more. There is a certain grimness there. Times8 are hard.

The interviewer also alludes to a poem that was either never completed, or has not survived: "His present literary project is to write a history of the Lebreton Flats, drawing from newspaper clippings, remembered tough guys, pool hall lore, etc. Part of his childhood and youth were spent in the area and he has an affinity for it, or at least its memory."

Still Life: Published as a broadside by *Anthos* Publications (Ottawa 1980), produced by Patrick White. A note along the bottom states "Design: Arthur II's Artforce." Produced in the spirit of the 1960s poster poems, "Still Life" coincides with the "Special/Double Ottawa Issue" of *Anthos* dedicated to Hawkins. The poster also includes a note identifying the "empty wine bottle" as "Barbera del Monferrato, Italy."

Simulated Linguistics: Previously unpublished. This poem, and the six that follow, are from a typescript held by Joanne Wiffen. The typescript contains these seven unpublished poems and ten additional poems included in *Dancing Alone* (the ten poems that follow "Suicide Note", not including "Sunrise: Villanelle"). Five of the poems from this typescript published in *Dancing Alone* were previously published in *The Canadian Forum* (June 1993). It is likely that these seven previously unpublished poems, as well as Wiffen's complete typescript, date approximately to 1993.

The Protestant Prince: See note regarding "Simulated Linguistics" in *Uncollected Poems.*

You Can Be Bought: See note regarding "Simulated Linguistics" in *Uncollected Poems.*

Travels of a Magus: See note regarding "Simulated Linguistics" in *Uncollected Poems.*

Cassandra's Xmas Poem: See note regarding "Simulated Linguistics" in *Uncollected Poems.*

Explanation # 3024: See note regarding "Simulated Linguistics" in *Uncollected Poems.*

Explanation # 3025: See note regarding "Simulated Linguistics" in *Uncollected Poems.*

King Kong Meets Godzilla: Originally published in *Peter F. Yacht Club* 4 (May 2005). Later published as above/ground press broadside

#318 (2013). The broadside includes a variant in the second stanza. The first two lines read: "Was it man's bombs made the sea's floor break? / & did that cause Godzilla to awake?"

My Next To Last Great Love: Published in *ottawater* 3 (January 2007) and *ottawater* 7 (January 2011).

Antecedents: Published in *ottawater* 3 (January 2007).

March Aubade: Published in *ottawater* 3 (January 2007).

Memories Memorial: Originally Published in *Peter F. Yacht Club* 11 (May 2008). Later published in the liner notes to *Dancing Alone: Songs of William Hawkins,* a collection of Hawkins's songs recorded in tribute by other artists The final track of the collection is a recording of Hawkins reading the poem. It is listed as "Memories: A Poem" on the tracklisting but printed as "Memories Memorial" in the liner notes.

In Memoriam (Sandra Jane Sutcliffe): Unpublished. Written 2 February 2013. Sandra Jane Sutcliffe (1953-2013) was a friend of Hawkins's.

Additional Works Cited

"Area poets hold read-in program." *Ottawa Citizen*. 16 February 1980. 38.

Frances, Wynne. "The Little Presses." *Canadian Literature* 33 (Summer 1967). 56-62.

Gessell, Paul. "Poet With a Past: William Hawkins returns with new work after long hiatus." *Ottawa Citizen*. 16 April 2005.

"Interview with William Hawkins." *Sparks Poetry Newsmagazine* 1 : 11 (January 1978): n.p.

"Jaycees honour young men's achievements." *Ottawa Citizen*. 24 November 1966. A3.

MacSkimming, Roy. "William Hawkins: A Unique Voice in Canadian Poetry." *Dancing Alone: Selected Poems*. By William Hawkins. Fredericton: Broken Jaw Press (Cauldron books 5), 2005. 11-18.

mclennan, rob. "The Return of William Hawkins, Ottawa's most dangerous poet." *rob mclennan's blog*. 17 May 2005. Web.

Weiselberger, Carl. "Of Dadaism, Nietzsche and Zen Buddhism." *Ottawa Citizen* 20 February 1962. 17.

Bibliography

Books

Shoot Low Sheriff, They're Riding Shetland Ponies! with Roy MacSkimming. Ottawa: [n.p.], 1964.

Two Longer Poems: the Seasons of Miss Nicky by Harry Howith and Louis Riel by William Hawkins. Toronto: Patrician Press, 1965.

Hawkins: Poems 1963-1965. Ottawa: Nil Press, 1966.

Ottawa Poems. Kitchener: Weed/Flower Press, 1966.

The Gift of Space: Selected Poems 1960/1970. Toronto: New Press, 1971.

The Madman's War. Ottawa: S.A.W. Publications, 1974.

Dancing Alone: Selected Poems. Fredericton: Broken Jaw Press (Cauldron Books 5), 2005.

the black prince of bank street. Ottawa: above/ground press, 2007.

Sweet & Sour Nothings. Ottawa: Apt. 9 Press, 2010.

Broadsides

"A Song of Flowers." Ottawa: Nil Press, [1962].

"King Kong Goes to Rotterdam." Ottawa: Nil Press, [1962].

"Postage Stamps." Ottawa: Nil Press, [1962].

"Rubber Boots: Canto 1." Ottawa: Nil Press, [1962].

"Two Short Ones." Ottawa: Nil Press, [1962].

"Zaap." Ottawa: Nil Press, [1962].

"One Glimpse of a Girl." PLIEGO-CANADA Broadside Series #42. Portland, Oregon: Wine Press, 1967.

"Still Life." Ottawa: Anthos Publications, 1980.

"Sheila Frances Louise." Ottawa: above/ground press broadside #206, 2004.

"Thinking of Cobwebs, for Nelson Ball." Ottawa: 1cent #362, 2005.

"King Kong Meets Godzilla." Ottawa: above/ground press broadside #318, 2013.

Periodical Publications

Alphabet, Anthos, The Canadian Forum, Delta, El Corno Emplumado, Evidence, Hyphid, IS, Island, LUV, ottawater, Peter F. Yacht Club, Something Else, Sparks, TISH, Volume 63, Weed.

See notes on individual poems for publication information.

Anthologies

Young Commonwealth Poets '65. Cardiff: William Heinemann Ltd., 1965.

New Wave Canada: The New Explosion in Canadian Poetry. Toronto: Contact Press, 1966.

Modern Canadian Verse. Toronto: Oxford UP, 1967.

Poetry of Relevance. Toronto: Methuen, 1970.

Northern Comfort. Ottawa: Commoners' Press, 1973.

Minutes of the Last Meeting. Toronto: room 302 books, Letters bookshop, Martin Garth Press, 1993.

Ground Rules: the best of the second decade of above/ground press. Ottawa: Chaudiere Books, 2013.

Audio and Video Recordings

Christopher's Movie Matinee. National Film Board of Canada, 1968.

Dancing Alone. Independent Release. 1997.

Dancing Alone: Songs of William Hawkins. True North Records, 2008.

The Children. *Time Capsule: The Unreleased 1960's Masters*. True North Records, 2013.

Poet's Acknowledgements

So many good people who inspired & helped me on the way to writing and publishing these poems....

Where would any of us be without parents? My wonderful mother, Fern Horsey, & her mother, Jenny Louisa Lockyear, started me off with James Whitcomb Riley, Robert Service, Rupert Brooke & the incomparable William Butler Yeats.

The next part is the toughest; I'm bound to leave someone out, so I start with an apology to everyone I've inadvertently omitted & ask for forgiveness.

I've got to start with Cameron Anstee, who not only published me earlier at his Apt. 9 Press but painstakingly compiled this collection, recovering many poems that I and everyone else had forgotten. Also rob mclennan of Chaudiere Books, publisher of this volume, who got me going with poetry again after a long absence when he edited my selected poems, *Dancing Alone*, for Joe Blades's Broken Jaw Press.

Having Roy MacSkimming & Chris Wells involved in this book, as they have been in practically everything I've published over the years, feels good. Must pay tribute to the late Andries Hamann, who taught me about being an artist. Harvey & Louise Glatt have been lifelong supporters & astute artistic advisers. David & Joanne Wiffen, Bruce Cockburn, Sneezy Waters, Sandy Crawley & Neville Wells were artistic mates in my song-writing years.

I've been influenced by too many great poets, Canadian & American as well as British & Irish, to list them all here. Irving Layton, in his introduction to his seminal *A Red Carpet for the Sun*, said the poet who had written these poems was dead. That applies here as well ... I think.

I also thank the late George Johnston, R.V. Rosewarne & W.R. (Bill) Roberts, as well as Nelson Ball, Noel Evans, Lois Wraight, Peter Bowie & Denis Faulkner, founder of Le Hibou.

I started writing poetry to gain the love & respect of Sheila Simpson, Deborah Arney, Constance Rand & other women who probably would appreciate not being mentioned.

And to my beautiful children, Andries, Jennifer & Cassandra, your youthful innocence was a constant inspiration.

William Hawkins
Ottawa 2015

Editor's Acknowledgements

Thank you to William Hawkins for your lifelong dedication to writing and art in Canada, and in Ottawa specifically. As a young poet in Ottawa, it was exhilarating to discover your work. Your kindness and generosity with me and with so many others deserves greater repayment than this book can provide.

For research help, I would like to extend my deepest thanks to Rod Anstee, Steven Artelle, Nelson Ball, Joe Blades, Marlys Chevrefils, David Collins, Richard Coxford, Sandy Crawley, jwcurry, Monique Desnoyers, Nicky Drumbolis, Noel Evans, Denis Faulkner, Harvey Glatt, Roy MacSkimming, rob mclennan, Ken Rockburn, Rick Stapleton, Christopher Wells, and Joanne Wiffen. William Hawkins's work as a poet and songwriter has been collected, catalogued, and documented by a number of peers and supporters over the years who have kept it from sliding into obscurity. This project could not have been completed without their labour. Thank you also to the editors and presses who published Bill's work. Thank you to rob, Christine, and Rose at Chaudiere Books for taking on this project (with extra gratitude to Christine for remarkable patience and care transforming this unwieldy manuscript into a beautifully designed book). Additional thanks to Nelson Ball and Roy MacSkimming for their moral support, fact-checking, and proof-reading.

Unending gratitude and love must also go to my partner Jenn, whose support and patience sustained my energy across this and countless other projects.

Cameron Anstee
Ottawa 2015

Index of Titles

William Hawkins was born in Ottawa in 1940. After side trips to the West Coast and Mexico, he resides in the capital, pursuing enlightenment or a reasonable alternative thereto. Hawkins worked as a truck driver, cook, journalist and musician before settling on the taxi profession as a means of preserving integrity and ensuring near-poverty. He is now retired. His work appeared in the seminal anthology *New Wave Canada: The New Explosion in Canadian Poetry* (Toronto: Contact Press, 1966) edited by Raymond Souster and *Modern Canadian Verse* (Toronto: Oxford, 1967) edited by A.J.M. Smith. His books include *Ottawa Poems* (Kitchener: Weed/Flower Press, 1966) and *The Madman's War* (Ottawa: S.A.W. Publications, 1974). Broken Jaw Press published his *Dancing Alone: Selected Poems* in 2005. Also an acclaimed songwriter, a tribute CD (*Dancing Alone: Songs of William Hawkins*) was released in 2008. In 2013, he was inducted into the VerseOttawa Hall of Honour.

Cameron Anstee lives and writes in Ottawa ON where he runs Apt. 9 Press and is pursuing a PhD studying Canadian literature at the University of Ottawa.

Colophon

Typeset in Joanna MT by Christine McNair in Adobe InDesign. Joanna was designed by Eric Gill in 1930, based on type originally cut by Granjon, and released by the Monotype Corporation in 1937. He created the typeface for the printing firm of Hague & Gill, which he formed to give his idle son-in-law an occupation, and named the design for his daughter. It is, as Gill himself described it, "a book face free from all fancy business."

WWW.CHAUDIEREBOOKS.COM

Library and Archives Canada Cataloguing in Publication

Hawkins, William, 1940-
[Poems]
The collected poems of William Hawkins / edited by Cameron Anstee.

Includes bibliographical references and index.
ISBN 978-1-928107-02-6 (bound)

I. Anstee, Cameron, editor II. Title.

PS8515.A895A17 2015 C811'.54 C2015-902119-7

Born in 1940 in Ottawa, Ontario, William Hawkins is one of the most important writers to emerge from Canada's capital. He published six books from 1964-1974, organized poetry readings at Ottawa's infamous Le Hibou Coffeehouse, wrote songs, and published widely in Canada's experimental little magazines before retreating into silence in the 1970s. *The Collected Poems of William Hawkins* prints his books alongside previously unpublished, uncollected, lost, and new work, presenting Hawkins's generous, defiant, idiosyncratic, and compelling poetry in its entirety.

"Everyone should read these poems."
— Bruce Cockburn
Dancing Alone, Broken Jaw Press, 2005.

"This is a grand addition to the William Hawkins revival. So good to have this comprehensive gathering of his poems. Bill's poems are imbued with his sardonic wit and the affecting poignancy of his plaintive existential cry. Bill was a dynamo in poetry and music circles in the 1960s and a mentor to grateful young musicians and poets including me. Cameron Anstee is to be praised for bringing this project to fruition. His meticulous notes on the poems are masterpieces of textual and bibliographic research. This is a truly wonderful book!"
— Nelson Ball

"William Hawkins is a rarity among poets: he assimilated early influences from Beat and Black Mountain sources to emerge with a unique poetic voice, ideally suited to his mordant, incisively ironic sensibility. This book, collating and documenting Hawkins's entire poetic output, is a signal literary event. It reminds us that, like Leonard Cohen, Hawkins is not only a wonderful songwriter but a gifted poet with much to tell the world. "
— Roy MacSkimming

$25.00 CAN/USD
ISBN 978-192810702-6
62500>
9 781928 107026

WWW.CHAUDIEREBOOKS.COM
Cover art by Chris Wells